Walk NUMBERS!

במדבר

In the wilderness

קרח   חקת
שלח לך אנשים   וירא בלק
בהעלתך את הנרות   פינחס בן אלעזר
נשא את ראש בני גרשון   המטות לבני ישראל
במדבר סיני באהל מועד   מסעי בני ישראל אשר יצאו

Jeffrey Enoch Feinberg, Ph.D.

illustrations by Kim Alan Moudy

Lederer Books
a division of
Messianic Jewish Publishers
Clarksville, Maryland

13 12 11 10   6 5 4 3

ISBN 13-978-1-880226-99-5
Library of Congress Catalog Control Number: 2002103556
Printed in the United States of America.

Walk NUMBERS! belongs to
the UMJC Special Collection
of recommended resources.

Lederer Books
a division of
Messianic Jewish Publishers
6120 Day Long Lane
Clarksville, Maryland 21029
(410) 531-6644

Distributed by
Messianic Jewish Resources International
Order line: (800) 410-7367
E-mail: lederer@messianicjewish.net
Website: www.messianicjewish.net

Acknowledgements

Special thanks to Pat, Jay, Kim, and Dan,
survivors of four books and counting!
JEF

Dedicated to all survivors of the wilderness,
the followers of Y'hoshua and Kalev
who keep their walks youthful
and join the new generation!

"So there was not left even one of them,
except Kalev the son of Y'funeh and Y'hoshua the son of Nun."
Numbers 26:65b

Preface

B'MIDBAR (*in the wilderness of*) Sinai, one generation dies and another generation honeymoons with God, grows up, and prepares itself to follow Him into the Land of Promise. The uniqueness of this nation stirs awe in the modern mind. God dwells in the nation's innermost circle, surrounded by His priests and hosts. When the divine cloud lifts, kohanim wrap God's mishkan (*dwelling*), sons of K'hat carry the holy items on their shoulders, and the nation journeys with God through the wilderness.

Twists and turns in obedience lengthen the journey. The old guard sends a representative minyan of spies to the scout the Land. Their slanderous report and subsequent failure to trust God condemns a generation to die in the wilderness. Slander can be a community killer. Miryam and Aharon will speak ill about Moshe's authority. Later, Korach and a rebel band of displaced priests and firstborns will launch simultaneous rebellions and attempt to expand the priesthood. Whereas Miryam will be personally punished by the LORD and put out of the camp for a week until her purity is restored, Korach's "mishkan" and those that spurn the LORD will go down alive into Sh'ol. The firstborns and men of stature who attempt to offer incense as a rival priesthood will be firebombed by the zeal of God to protect His glory.

In Sefer SH'MOT (*Book of Exodus/names*), God initially greets complaints about food and water with the provision of manna. But now, repeated complaints about food, water, and manna bring poisonous vipers. Mysteriously, only the bitten who look upon a raised-up serpent made of bronze will live. God Himself had ordered Moshe to make and raise up the bronze serpent, and God Himself mysteriously heals those who observe His statute.

The disobedient generation appears to die off in a flash of time. One moment, Korach's rebellion dominates the text. In the next parashah, CHUKAT (*statute of*) the red cow addresses cleansing the camp of corpse contamination. In the same verse, the congregation moves from the spot of ritual cleansing after Korach's rebellion through perhaps eighteen rest spots in eighteen years and comes to Kadesh where it pauses for nineteen more years until Miryam dies (Num. 20:1; cf. 12:15-13:3, 14:45, 33:18-36). So begins the fortieth year. The nineteenth and very next stop at Mount Hor, Aharon dies. Death provides an atonement. The new generation shakes off the sins of the fathers and stands ready to enter the Land of Promise.

It should not go unnoticed that there are nineteen generations from Adam to Terach (the father who is cut off from Avraham his son who will become the father of the millennium). Nor should it go unnoticed that Yisra'el has nineteen idolatrous kings before the Assyrians haul a minyan of tribes off to destruction, exile, assimilation, and death as a nation.

The prophets foretell a new covenant with Yisra'el as well as with Y'hudah (Jer. 31:31-34). Y'hoshua and Kalev, God's witnesses who stood against the minyan that slandered the Land, actually grow up to lead the new generation across the Yarden. Thus, continuities link the honeymoon generation, the two faithful spies, and the leaders who live to enter the Land. Could ancient Yisra'el be resurrected? Let it be remembered that in Romans 11:15, Rav Sha'ul writes, "For if their casting Yeshua aside means reconciliation of the world, what will their accepting mean? It will be life from the dead!"

JEF
3/10/02

Walk NUMBERS*!*

Each section begins with a "doodle" of a scene from the portion. Embedded in the scene, cursive Hebrew letters spell out the portion name. Next comes an entertaining synopsis in rhyme. Now on to the meat of the Word! Sub-section titles scope out the flow of the story across the Torah portion, the Haftarah, and related B'rit Chadashah readings. Finally, the phrase at the bottom of the page focuses the reader on the "key idea."

The *Hiker's Log* offers a cumulative summary of what has happened to date in the story, a hint at what lies ahead, a box capsulizing the summary, and a second box listing the people, places, and events to come.

For Hebrew lovers, *Compass Work* spells out the portion name letter by letter. Scripture supplies the context for this name, and the first verse is analyzed phrase by phrase. Related Words show how the root word gets used in everyday speech.

Starting with the Rishon, each segment of Torah is featured on its own page. The topic verse is quoted, key ideas are emphasized, and challenging discussion questions stimulate contemplation. Please note that the footer at the bottom of each page references the entire segment under discussion. It is recommended that the reader consult the Scripture before reading the commentary for each particular segment.

The name *Meanderings* suggests how our journey through Torah now turns to related "excursion side-trips" in the Haftarah (*Prophets*) and B'rit Chadashah (*New Covenant/New Testament*). The format matches that of the Torah sub-sections. Like the maftir, these pages feature a quote from the end of the passage being studied. Due to limited space, ideas are compact. For

Features

readers desiring to meditate on these passages, a number of cross-references (cf.) are provided. (*Please note: Selections from the B'rit Chadashah reflect efforts to complement the annual reading cycle for the Torah and Haftarah. It is not suggested that the current selections are the only readings for a given portion.*)

The *Oasis* has two segments: *Talk Your Walk*, a conclusion drawn from the portion; and *Walk Your Talk*, a personal application. Remarks in *Journey's End* sum up all of Numbers.

Hebrew names for Torah portions, people, places, and terms of interest are sprinkled throughout the text to add cultural context to the story. The italicized English meaning generally follows in parentheses; otherwise, check the **Glossary**. Whenever verse numbers vary, the references for the Tanakh are given in parentheses with the Hebrew תנ״ך to identify them.

To use this volume as a daily devotional, the following reading plan is suggested. Begin just after Shabbat to prepare for the next week's reading, typically listed on any Jewish calendar.

Sunday	*Hiker's Log* and *Compass Work* (overview)
Monday	*Rishon* and *Sheni* Sections of the Torah portion
Tuesday	*Shlishi* and *R'vi'i* Sections
Wednesday	*Chamishi* and *Shishi* Sections
Thursday	*Shvi'i* and *Maftir* Sections
Friday	*Meanderings* (Haftarah and B'rit Chadashah)
Saturday	*Oasis* (summary and application)

Readers with less time might browse each chapter as one might page through a magazine. The *Hiker's Log* and *Oasis* segments offer the best overview.

Table of

Contents

במדבר, in the wilderness,
count, count, count
every soldier twenty years and up
here on the Mount.
Count 'em tribe by tribe,
every Israelite son.
Separate the Levites
to get priestly work done!

Circle the ark,
Levites camp near Me.
Exchange all firstborns
for the Levites you see.
Count 22,000,
leaving 273.
For the rest, pay 5 shekels—
My redemption fee!

Walk B'MIDBAR!
1:1-4:20

In the wilderness

TORAH—Numbers 1:1-4:20

HAFTARAH—Hosea 1:10-2:20(2:1-22 תנ״ך)

B'RIT CHADASHAH—Romans 9:22-33

In the Wilderness, a Priestly Nation Arises

← Looking Back

B'REISHEET (*in the beginning*), God creates perfection! But man disobeys, paradise crashes, and the world fragments into nations. Thus begins a long journey to return to God's Presence and walk in covenant with Him.

v'Eleh SH'MOT (*and these are names*) of seventy sons of Ya'akov. Reunited as a family in Egypt, they grow in numbers, then suffer slavery until God redeems them. Yisra'el becomes a kingdom of priests—called to build God's dwelling, unite as a nation, and bring all nations to covenant with the God of Avraham, Yitzchak, and Ya'akov!

vaYIKRA ADONAI (*and the LORD called*) to Moshe, and later the nation, to draw near to Him. Under God's protective covering, Yisra'el abides as a holy nation in the manifest Presence of a holy God. The nation elevates kohanim to abide in close proximity to God and to devote exceptional attention to matters of ritual purity, a

B'REISHEET, in the beginning,
God creates Paradise,
but we fail to rest.
God begins again with Avraham
and his family of covenant faith.

And these are the SH'MOT,
names of the children of Yisra'el,
who go to Egypt to survive famine.
Our numbers grow. We're enslaved.
But God delivers us from bondage
and forms us into a nation!

VAYIKRA—and He calls us to
become holy, a kingdom of priests
with God at the heart of our camp.

The Land of Promise lies ahead,
but we wander in the wilderness,
B'MIDBAR Sinai . . .

Log

necessary state for abiding in the presence of a holy God.

A priestly nation arises B'MIDBAR (*in the wilderness of*) Sinai, and all stand up to be counted for the LORD! God says to number the army of the LORD of Hosts. Then He surrounds His dwelling with an inner circle of priests and their assistants, to safeguard it from encroachment by those in a state of ritual impurity. The rest of the house of Yisra'el encircles the Levites, camping under the banners of their respective tribes.

Following the pattern established by the theophany at Mt. Sinai, God speaks to Moshe. Moshe then passes on God's instruction to Aharon and his sons and, in turn, to all the sons of Yisra'el encamped at the foot of

In B'MIDBAR . . .

The Key People are Moshe (*Moses*); Aharon (*Aaron*); heads of the tribes (1:5-15); Aharon's sons Nadav (*Nadab*), Avihu (*Abihu*), El'azar (*Eleazer*), and Itamar (*Ithamar*); Levi's sons Gershon, K'hat (*Kohath*), M'rari (*Merari*), all their sons; and firstborn males.

The Scene is B'MIDBAR Sinai, in the wilderness of Sinai.

Main Events include a census for the army; tent arrangement in the camp; Levites replacing firstborns as God's own, then set apart for tabernacle service; Kohathites counted; and instructions for Aharon and sons to cover holy items, so Kohathites carrying them don't see them and die.

Mount Sinai. Eventually, the heritage passes on to us, as we continue wandering *in the wilderness* . . .

The Trail Ahead ➡

The Path

וידבר יהוה אל משה

במדבר סיני באהל מועד

באחד לחדש השני

בשנה השנית

לצאתם מארץ מצרים לאמר

—במדבר א/א

	ר	בַּ	דְ	מְ	בְּ
letter:	reish	bet	dalet	mem	bet
sound:	R	**Bah**	D	Mee	B'

in the wilderness = B'MIDBAR = במדבר

Work

And spoke the LORD	*va-y'daber ADONAI*	וַיְדַבֵּר יְהוָה
to Moses	*el-Moshe*	אֶל־מֹשֶׁה
<u>in the wilderness of</u> Sinai	*b'midbar Seenai*	בְּמִדְבַּר סִינַי
in the Tent of Meeting	*b'Ohel Mo'ed*	בְּאֹהֶל מוֹעֵד
on (day) one (of)	*b'echad*	בְּאֶחָד
the month the second	*la-chodesh ha-sheni*	לַחֹדֶשׁ הַשֵּׁנִי
in the year the second	*ba-shanah ha-shenit*	בַּשָּׁנָה הַשֵּׁנִית
of going-out-their	*l'tsetam*	לְצֵאתָם
from the land of Egypt,	*me-erets Mitsrayim*	מֵאֶרֶץ מִצְרַיִם
saying . . .	*lemor*	לֵאמֹר׃

—Numbers 1:1

Related Words

desert, wilderness	*midbar*	מִדְבָּר
the Desert Generation	*dor ha-midbar*	דוֹר הַמִּדְבָּר
oasis	*n'veh midbar*	נְוֵה מִדְבָּר
desert-like, wild, barren, desolate	*midbari*	מִדְבָּרִי
wilderness, desolation	*midbarioot*	מִדְבָּרִיּוּת
uncultivated, uncivilized (lit. beast taught of desert)	*pere limood midbar*	פֶּרֶא לְמוּד מִדְבָּר
voice crying in the wilderness, unheeded call	*kol kore ba-midbar*	קוֹל קוֹרֵא בַּמִּדְבָּר

Hit the Trail!

Count the Army!

> ❝ ADONAI *spoke to Moshe in the Sinai Desert, in the tent of meeting, on the first day of the second month of the second year after they had left the land of Egypt. He said, "Take a census ..."* ❞ —Num. 1:1-2a

Midbar (*wilderness*) ahead, ADONAI-Tsva'ot (*the* LORD *of Hosts/Armies*) reorganizes Yisra'el into a military camp. God orders a census in the second year on the new moon of Iyar, two weeks after Passover. In contrast to the count at Sinai by half-shekel ransom (Ex. 30:12, 38:26), this count lifts up individuals l'gul'g'lotam (*by their skulls*, Num. 1:2).

ADONAI elevates each tribe's nasi (*lifted up one*, i.e. *chieftain/clan leader*) by name, starting with Elitsur, son of firstborn R'uven. Called rashei alfei Yisra'el (*heads of the thousands of Israel*), the n'si'im rule as *clan leaders* over the families (Num. 1:5-16). They count all those eligible for military service, males over twenty years of age, by clan and by fathers' house (Num. 1:2-3).

Count the hosts by name.

Each nasi oversees his own list of names (Num. 1:17-18). What takes David over nine months to count (2 Sam. 24:8; cf. Num. 10:11), Moshe and Aharon delegate and complete in under 20 days!

? *Read Mt. 27:33 and 1 Cor. 15:20. Yeshua was offered as a ransom at Gulgolta, "Place of the Skull," then raised up as the firstfruits of the dead. Explain why we must be ransomed before our names can be listed in the Book of Life.*

List All but Levites

❝ The men twenty years old and over who were subject to military service were recorded by name, family and clan, starting with the descendants of Re'uven, Isra'el's firstborn . . . ❞   *—Numbers 1:20*

The census of soldiers eligible for military service commences! Totals of 603,550 indicate the nature of the delegation process, with counts rounded to the nearest thousands, hundreds, fifties, and tens (cf. Ex. 18:21).

Starting with R'uven, the firstborn, and concluding with Naftali, the last son born to the second wife's concubine, Torah lists totals for each tribe as follows (Num. 1:21-43):

R'uven 46,500, Shim'on 59,300, Gad 45,650;

Y'hudah 74,600, Yissakhar 54,400, Z'vulun 57,400;

Efrayim 40,500, M'nasheh 32,200, Binyamin 35,400;

Dan 62,700, Asher 41,500, Naftali 53,400.

These lists follow birth order and mothers' status to some extent. Sons of Leah come first, Rachel's offspring next, and concubines' children last. The exception comes when Gad, a larger military power, replaces third-born Levi, whose priestly tribe does not serve in the military.

Levites do not count as part of the military.

No one counts the Levites, excluded from this census as well as from the judgment falling on this generation (Num. 1:47, 26:64). As a result, Levites survive to become great-grandfathers passing on their priestly heritage.

Read Num. 1:47-49 and 26:63-65; cf. Ex. 32:26-29. Explain the tie between obedience and long life in the Land. Also describe the role of great-grandparents in shaping priestly values for society at large.

Encircle God's Dwelling

❝ *ADONAI said to Moshe and Aharon, "The people of Isra'el are to set up camp by clans, each man with his own banner . . . around the tent of meeting, but at a distance."* ❞   —*Numbers 2:1-2*

Each clan encamps in its own designated spot, 3000 feet from the tabernacle [Num. 2:2; cf. Num. 35:5, Josh. 3:4, Tanch. 9, Rashi]. In the inner circle, the Levites guard all approaches from encroachment (Num. 1:53).

Call the faithful to surround the ark!

The tribe of Y'hudah faces east, toward the sunrise, ready to march first (Num. 2:3-9). Ya'akov had prophesied a leadership role for this fourth-born son and his scepter (Gen. 49:10). Now listed first, the tribe numbers 74,600, greatest of all! The Mekhilta [Beshallah, 6] credits Nachson, Nasi of Y'hudah, as first to enter the parting sea.

With marching orders now set, Yisra'el will soon leave Mt. Sinai for the first time (Num. 10:11-12)! Thus begin fifty spaces in the Torah scroll's Hebrew lettering, from v'<u>nasa</u> (*journey*, Num. 2:17) to vay'hi bi<u>nso'a</u> ha-aron (*when the ark would journey*, Num. 10:35). These gaps parallel the pauses in the journey B'MIDBAR (*in the wilderness of*) Sinai, en route to the Land of Promise!

?• *Talmud relates the journey of the ark through the wilderness as God's Word that arises and goes before His people [Shabb. 115a, b]. Comment on the congregational experience of processing Torah as part of the Shabbat liturgy.*

Consecrate the Inner Circle

> ❝ These are the descendants of Aharon and Moshe as of the day when ADONAI spoke with Moshe on Mount Sinai. ❞
>
> —Numbers 3:1

Says the LORD, "Assign the L'vi'im to Aharon and his sons" (Num. 3:9). No longer do firstborns perform religious functions for households; now kohanim, assisted by Levites, perform these functions for the whole nation.

Installing Aharon's sons as kohanim requires mille yadam (ordination, lit. *filling their hands*, Num. 3:3; cf. Ex. 28:41, Lev. 8:33). These m'shuchim (*anointed ones*) now receive assistance from the Levites, who safeguard the tabernacle and all its furnishings. The L'vi'im perform their duties for all the congregation, la'avod et avodat ha-mishkan (*to do the work/service/worship of the dwelling*, Num. 3:7).

Only Aharon and his sons, El'azar and Itamar, are kohanim. All other Levites are n'tunim n'tunim (formally *given over*, Num. 3:9) to the kohanim in place of the firstborns.

Only kohanim are holy.

Aharon and sons must guard their priesthood; any zar (*stranger*, i.e. non-priest) who encroaches shall die (Num. 3:10)!

? Read Num. 3:13. God says: Hikdashti (I made holy/sanctified to myself) every firstborn of Yisra'el on the day the Egyptian firstborns died. Review Num. 3:9. Explain why the Levites are dedicated, not sanctified.

Now, Count the Levites

" ADONAI said to Moshe in the Sinai Desert, "Take a census of the tribe of Levi by clans and families. Count every male a month old or over." "

—Numbers 3:14-15

P'kod . . . tif'k'dem ("*you shall most certainly count*") the tribe of Levi, every male over thirty days, God commands (Num. 3:15). Firstborns under a month old are not yet eligible for pidyon ha ben (*redemption of the firstborn*).

Count the L'vi'im, starting with the firstborn.

In the army census, tribal leaders oversee the writing of names (Num. 1:2, 17-18); God commands Moshe himself to record this count (Num. 3:16). The count includes 7500 Gershonites, 8600 Kohathites, and 6200 Merarites. The listed total of 22,000 L'vi'im does not include the 300 firstborns who can redeem themselves, but not others [Rashi].

Each clan receives a designated campsite, as well as assigned responsibilities for maintaining specific parts of the tabernacle and its furnishings. Camping in front of the tabernacle on the east toward the sunrise are Moshe and Aharon with his two sons. On behalf of the people, they take charge of the Holy Place. Any zar (*stranger*) who encroaches holy ground must be put to death!

? *Notable clan heads within K'hat include his firstborn, Amram (father of Aharon and Moshe), and his second-born, Yitzhar (father of Korach). Explain Korach's jealousy over exclusion from the inner circle (Num. 16:1-3).*

Levites for Firstborns

❝ ADONAI said to Moshe, "Register all the firstborn males of the people of Isra'el a month old and over, and determine how many there are." ❞

—Numbers 3:40

Firstborns counted by Moshe exceed the L'vi'im by 273 (Num. 3:39, 43). A redemption price of five shekels for each unpaired firstborn is paid to the kohanim, ka'asher tsivah ADONAI et-Moshe (*as the LORD commanded Moses*, Num. 3:51).

Reorganize from a nation of households to a national household.

Shekels are paid according to standard weight measurements. Since coinage awaits the seventh century BCE, shekels designate a weight measure, perhaps the silver content of a silver dollar. The five shekel amount matches the value suggested for a boy one month to five years old (Lev. 27:6).

Exchange includes not only the L'vi'im for firstborns, but also cattle for cattle (Num. 3:45). Exchanged cattle do not become personal possessions, but rather property of the sanctuary. By contrast, the exchange releases the firstborns' cattle from their sacred status, enabling them to become the personal property of the firstborns.

Infants who are under 30 days old that die receive no mourning rites [MK 24b]. Study Num. 3:12-13. Comment on whether these sons, not yet considered viable and thus not yet redeemed, have lives. To whom do they belong?

Raise Up the Kohathites

❝ ADONAI said to Moshe and Aharon, "Take a census of the descendants of K'hat, who are . . . descendants of Levi, by clans and families, all those from thirty to fifty years old . . ." ❞   —Numbers 4:1-3a

A second census of the L'vi'im, beginning with the Kohathites, counts all men eligible for ministry (Num. 4:3). The tsava (*work force*) requires strenuous work activity, so an age limit of 30 to 50 is set for those performing assigned tasks at the Ohel Mo'ed (*Tent of Meeting*).

Double-count those doing sacred service.

Sons of K'hat transport the most sacred objects. But they are restricted from touching or even gazing upon the holy objects they carry, lest they die (Num. 4:15, 20).

Procedures call for the kohanim, Aharon and sons, to enter first and cover the most holy furnishings and utensils. Specific details explain which of the finely crafted coverings to use over each item (ark, table, incense altar, m'norah, altar of ascent offerings, and laver). El'azar is personally responsible for the oil for the light, the incense, the continuing grain offering, and the anointing oil.

Only after all the items are covered can the sons of K'hat enter the mishkan to shoulder the sacred objects on the march.

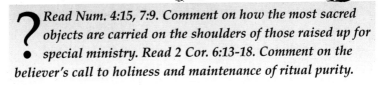

? *Read Num. 4:15, 7:9. Comment on how the most sacred objects are carried on the shoulders of those raised up for special ministry. Read 2 Cor. 6:13-18. Comment on the believer's call to holiness and maintenance of ritual purity.*

Limits of the Inner Circle

" . . . but the descendants of K'hat are not to go in and look at the holy things as they are being covered; if they do, they will die. "

—*Numbers 4:20*

Approaching the ark can be lethal! L'vi'im encamp around the mishkan edut (*dwelling of testimony*), lest the unholy encroach and kindle the wrath of the LORD (Num. 1:53, 8:19). Even Kohathites will die if they gaze upon the holy items, k'valla (*for as long as it takes to swallow*) (Fox, Num. 4:20).

Protect Kohathites for their time of service.

Thus, kohanim receive the sternest of warnings to pack all transport items thoroughly and carefully, so they do not expose the sons of K'hat to the dangers of encroachment.

Under the supervision of El'azar, the kohanim bundle six packages for transport: the ark with its screen; the table with bread; the m'norah with its tongs, trays, and oil vessels; the golden altar; the altar of ascent offerings; and utensils not assigned to particular furnishings [Budd, p. 50].

Perhaps to assure the Kohathites that stipulations protect them (and do not degrade them), scripture elevates the Kohathites for service ahead of their firstborn counterparts, the Gershonites.

? *Read Num. 4:18. Only the Kohathites, not the Gershonites or Merarites, are in mortal danger of karet (being cut off). Explain why the LORD warns Moshe and Aharon, and not the Kohathites, concerning this danger.*

Inner Circle Renewed   *Meander*

> ❝ *I will betroth you to me in faithfulness, and you will know* ADONAI. ❞
>
> —*Hosea 2:20(22 תג״י)*

Hoshea prophesies a great day in the end (Hos. 1:10-11(2:1-2 תג״י)), though Yisra'el first will bring disgrace by acting the harlot (2:2-7 (4-9 תג״י)). She suffers terrible consequences for her faithlessness (2:8-13(10-15 תג״י)). But restoration follows (2:14-20 (16-22 תג״י))! Yisra'el sings again as in her youth, when God brought her from Egypt to the midbar to speak to her heart (2:14-15(16-17 תג״י)).

Remember that Hoshea shares in Yisra'el's history by marrying Gomer, a prostitute who mothers three children: Yizra'el (*God will sow*) fathered by Hosea; and Lo-Ruchamah (*No Mercy*) and Lo-'Ammi (*Not My People*), both fathered by other lovers of the prostitute. But Hoshea cannot reject his children! In this moment, God shows Hoshea that He cannot reject Yisra'el either.

A changed nature for a renewed covenant!

Thus, God renews His covenant in faithfulness and promises to change Yisra'el's very nature [Hos. 2:17(18 תג״י), JPS, p. 984, nl-l]. She will be made faithful and know the LORD (2:20(22 תג״י))!

> **?** *Distinguish between husbands and masters (2:16(18 תג״י)), and consider why 2:19-20(21-22 תג״י) is recited at weddings. Read 2:21-23(23-25 תג״י); then explain how God will sow His people in the Land and embrace outsiders, too.*

> ❝ As the Tanakh puts it, "Look, I am laying in Tziyon a stone that will make people stumble, a rock that will trip them up. But he who rests his trust on it will not be humiliated." ❞   —Rom. 9:33

Paul quotes Hosea to say that Lo-'Ammi becomes God's people (Ro. 9:25-26). The terrible consequences of faithlessness result in Yisra'el being carved down from being countless as the grains of the sand (Hos. 2:1) to little more than a remnant (Ro. 9:27-29). Still, God promises to restore faithfulness and make it a constitutional reality that's bestowed graciously upon the gentiles as well (Ro. 9:30)!

B'MIDBAR Sinai, the priestly tribe replaced the firstborns in the inner circle surrounding the tabernacle, as a direct result of their faithfulness to God when the rest of Yisra'el whored after Ba'al (Ex. 32).

Those who suffer for their faith will receive mercy.

Now God brings others near (Lo-Ruchamah and Lo-'Ammi)—not simply as a result of Yisra'el's faithlessness, but also "to make known the riches of his glory to those who are objects of his mercy . . . that is, to us, whom he called not only from among the Jews but also from among the Gentiles" (Ro. 9:23-24)!

> ❓ *Read Ro. 9:22, 31-32. Consider whether it makes sense to say that there are both humble and proud ways to obey Torah. Whom does God place in His inner circle? Must one have some righteousness to be shown mercy?*

Talk Your Walk . . .

In the Torah, God directs Moshe to number those eligible for military service. L'vi'im are numbered in a separate census, and those eligible for service are counted in yet another, separate tally. L'vi'im are exchanged for firstborns and become God's property, gifted to the kohanim for national service. The kohanim they serve are doubly raised up, as holy to the LORD. As the nation's inner circle, priests and Levites encamp closest to the mishkan (*dwelling*), charged with the sacred duty to safeguard the camp from encroachment by those who are not ritually pure.

God calls mankind to draw near to him.

In the Haftarah, Hosea's house embodies the fallen state of corporate Yisra'el. In obedience, he marries a faithless prostitute, who fathers three children—one of whom is his and two others sired by faithless lovers. Even so, neither Hosea nor God will abandon those born outside the covenant relationship. In grace, God promises to change Yisra'el's heart and renew the covenant as in the earliest day of freedom from Egypt.

The B'rit Chadashah offers renewal of the covenant relationship to all mankind. God brings near those whom strict justice would spurn. Lo-Ruchamah (*no mercy*) and Lo-'Ammi (*not My people*) are ushered into a heavenly inner circle as New Covenant kohanim (cf. Heb. 10:19). In this way, God makes known his mercy to the gentiles, those born outside the covenant!

Oasis

. . . Walk Your Talk

Are you called to God's inner circle? B'MIDBAR (*in the wilderness of*) Sinai, only those properly anointed and clothed can enter the holy courts of the LORD. The average Israelite (or even Levite) is excluded from looking upon the holy furniture, let alone entering to speak to the LORD with prayers and petitions. Only Moshe, on behalf of the nation, and later the Kohen Gadol on Yom Kippur, can enter the holy Presence of God.

But through faithless behaviors, Yisra'el and all mankind collectively drive ADONAI from His camp. God no longer manifests His Presence among us in visible ways. In the New Covenant, however, God graciously provides a newer and better means for all to draw near to Him. Anyone clothed in the robes of the Anointed One can draw near to God, at any time! The book of Hebrews tells us, "Trusting is being confident of what we hope for, convinced about things we do not see,"

Answer the call to draw near to God!

(Heb. 11:1). Faith opens the way for everyone to trust and stand in the Presence of the living God. Rejoice sing, pray, and petition! The King of the Universe has given you this high and holy privilege!

 **Shabbat Shalom!**

נָשֹׂא means <u>elevate</u>—
lift up your face!
Be counted for service
in the Holy Place.
Gershon takes curtains,
M'rari the base,
K'hat shoulders holy things
from space to space.

No wine or haircuts
on a Nazirite vow.
When Aaron gives his blessing,
lift your face and say, "WOW!"
Twelve tribes come with offerings,
twelve days they rejoice
'til the sanctuary's ready
and Moshe hears God's voice!

Walk NASO!
4:21-7:89

Elevate!

TORAH—Numbers 4:21-7:89
- 1st Raised Up to Serve—Numbers 4:21-23
- 2nd Census Complete!—Numbers 4:38-39
- 3rd Purifying the Camp—Numbers 5:1-2
- 4th Vows and Blessing—Numbers 5:11, 15a
- 5th The Tabernacle Sanctified—Numbers 7:1
- 6th All Leaders Participate—Numbers 7:42-43a
- 7th Identical Offerings—Numbers 7:72-73a
- Maftir The Voice of God—Numbers 7:89

HAFTARAH—Judges 13:2-25
- Shimshon Elevates the Nation—Judges 13:24-25

B'RIT CHADASHAH—John 12:20-36
- Yeshua Elevates the Nations—John 12:36a

Lift Up the Nation!

← Looking Back

B'REISHEET (*in the beginning*), God creates perfection! But man disobeys, and paradise crashes. Thus begins a long journey to return to the old days when man walked with God.

v'Eleh SH'MOT (*and these are names*) of seventy from Ya'akov's family, reunited in Egypt. With a mighty hand, God delivers us from slavery, that we might serve Him. We grow into a kingdom of priests—instructed to build God's dwelling, unite as a nation, and call all nations to covenant with the God of Avraham, Yitzchak, and Ya'akov!

vaYIKRA ADONAI (*and the LORD called*) to Moshe to draw near to Him. Under God's protective covering, Yisra'el abides as a holy nation in the manifest Presence of a holy God. The nation elevates kohanim to abide in close proximity to God and to devote exceptional attention to matters of ritual purity. God not only frees His people from slavery, but causes us to walk with our heads held high!

B'MIDBAR, *in the wilderness of Sinai, number the army and arrange the tents.*
Count Levites separately—all who can serve in the LORD's Tabernacle.
Count on K'hat to shoulder the holiest items.

Next, elevate Gershon—yes, NASO *Levi's firstborn for special service.*
Count M'rari too, so each clan gets elevated to serve!

B'MIDBAR (*in the wilderness of*) Sinai, God surrounds His Presence with priests, their assistants, and then with the rest of the house of Yisra'el. Following the pattern established at Mt. Sinai, God speaks to Moshe, who then passes instruction on to Aharon and his sons and, in

Log

turn, to all Yisra'el. Eventually, the heritage passes on to us, as we wander in the wilderness.

To advance to the Land, God orders a census of his earthly hosts, the army of Yisra'el. L'vi'im are not included; rather, they are counted in a separate census, with those age 30-50 counted a second time for the special service of tabernacle ministry.

Lift up the nation, Moshe is told, and raise up the Levites to do specific tasks. God calls the kohanim to the inner circle, with sons of K'hat just outside that circle. These Kohathites enter the most holy sphere only after the kohanim wrap the holiest items which reside in the Holy of Holies and the Holy Place. But to preclude problems of sibling rivalry,

In NASO . . .

The Key People are Moshe (*Moses*); all the Levites—sons of Gershon, M'rari (*Merari*), and K'hat (*Kohath*); the unclean; jealous husbands and their wives; Nazirites; Aharon (*Aaron*); and leaders of all the tribes.

The Scene is the wilderness of Sinai.

The Main Events include tasks for the Gershonites and Merarites; census totals for Levites; instructions to keep tsara'at (*infection*) out of the camp; law of jealousy; Nazirite vows; Aaronic benediction; altar dedicated; offerings of the tribal princes; donations for Levites; and Moshe entering the tabernacle to hear the LORD speak.

each clan of Levi will be elevated for its own special service. So the LORD commands: NASO (*elevate!*) Gershon, firstborn among his brothers, and lift him up first of all . . .

The Trail Ahead

The Path

וַיְדַבֵּר יְהֹוָה אֶל מֹשֶׁה לֵּאמֹר

נָשֹׂא אֶת רֹאשׁ בְּנֵי גֵרְשׁוֹן

גַּם הֵם לְבֵית אֲבֹתָם

לְמִשְׁפְּחֹתָם

—במדבר ד/כא-כב

	א	שׂ	נָ
letter:	alef	sin	nun
sound:	(silent)	**So**	Nah

elevate! = NASO = נָשֹׂא

Work

The Legend

And spoke the Lord	*va-y'daber* ADONAI	וַיְדַבֵּר יְהוָה
to Moses, saying,	*el-Moshe lemor*	אֶל־מֹשֶׁה לֵּאמֹר׃
"<u>Elevate</u> (the) head(s) (take a census of)	*naso et-rosh*	נָשֹׂא אֶת־רֹאשׁ
(the) sons of Gershon,	*b'nei Gershon*	בְּנֵי גֵרְשׁוֹן
also them,	*gam-hem*	גַּם־הֵם
by the house of fathers-their	*l'veit avotam*	לְבֵית אֲבֹתָם
by families-their."	*l'mish'p'chotam*	לְמִשְׁפְּחֹתָם׃

—*Numbers 4:21-22*

Related Words

to carry, bear, lift, raise, transfer, take, endure	*nasa*	נָשָׂא
to find favor in the eyes of	*nasa chen b'einei*	נָשָׂא חֵן בְּעֵינֵי
to please, find grace before	*nasa chehsed lifnei*	נָשָׂא חֶסֶד לִפְנֵי
high, lofty, exalted	*nisa*	נִשָּׂא
to look about, lift his eyes	*nasa et einav*	נָשָׂא אֶת עֵינָיו
to raise his voice, burst into tears	*nasa kolo*	נָשָׂא קוֹלוֹ
to boast, be proud, lift his head	*nasa rosho*	נָשָׂא רֹאשׁוֹ
when you elevate (take a census) (Ex. 30:12)	*ki tisa*	כִּי תִשָּׂא
take a census (elevate the head of the people)	*nasa et rosh ha-anashim*	נָשָׂא אֶת רֹאשׁ הָאֲנָשִׁים
The Lord lift up	*yisa* ADONAI	יִשָּׂא יְהוָה
His face to you (Num. 6:26)	*panav eleicha*	פָּנָיו אֵלֶיךָ

Hit the Trail!

Raised Up to Serve

❝ ADONAI said to Moshe, "Take a census of the descendants of Gershon also, by clans and families; count all those between thirty and fifty years old . . . serving in the tent of meeting."❞ —Num. 4:21-23

Although Gershon is Amram's firstborn, K'hat received the first job assignment (Num. 4:1-20). Gershon is still honored, however, by placement at the head of this new parashah [Abarbanel].

Like K'hat, Gershon and M'rari help transport the tabernacle.

Gershon's duties concern the physical work of dismantling, loading onto wagons, and reassembling the cloth, fabric, and skins that cover and enclose the mishkan [Ashley, p. 107].

Kohathites have already removed the holiest items, which they themselves shoulder. Now Gershonites remove the coverings, exposing the framework. Merarites enter next, doing the heaviest work of dismantling, packing, and unpacking frameworks for the mishkan and outer court.

Itamar, son of Aharon the kohen, supervises the work of the Gershonites and the Merarites. He assigns particular loads to specific persons by name (Num. 4:27-28, 32-33).

❓ Seven times Levites are called to avodah (service). Repetitions are carefully arranged to introduce (Num. 4:3, 23, 30), to summarize (Num. 4:35, 39, 43), and to summarize the summary (Num. 4:47). Comment on the nature of service.

Census Complete!

> **❝** *The census of the descendants of Gershon, by their clans and families, all those between thirty and fifty years old who were part of the corps serving in the tent of meeting . . .* **❞** —*Numbers 4:38-39*

With tasks specified for K'hat, Gershon, and M'rari, the count of Levites 30-50 years old gets recorded. Once again, Kohathites come first; but the segment breaks so that firstborn Gershon continues the count here in a featured position at the start of the sheni segment.

It makes sense logically to record all Levites together. Indeed, Sephardic tradition includes the Kohathite total of 2750 in this reading (Num. 4:34-37). Ashkenazim, however, break the segment between the counts for K'hat and Gershon.

It appears that maintaining the honor of the firstborn plays a role in how the record reads. The breaks in the story line, both from week to week (across portions) and from reader to reader (across segments) minimize the temptation to sibling rivalry.

Levitical census yields 8580 ready to serve.

Thus all counts are complete: Gershonites, 2630; Merarites, 3200; and the total of all Levites, including Kohathites, 8580 (Num. 4:40, 44, 48).

? *Torah states that the Levites are counted at the command of the LORD alone, al pi ADONAI (Num. 3:16, 39, 51; 4:37, 41, 45, 49). Milgrom [p. xxxi] says this septenary repetition emphasizes its specialness. What specialness?*

Purifying the Camp

" *ADONAI said to Moshe, "Order the people of Isra'el to expel . . . everyone with tzara'at, everyone with a discharge and whoever is unclean because of touching a corpse."* **"**

—*Numbers 5:1-2*

Holiness must be maintained in the camp where God dwells (Num. 5:3). A tsaru'a (*one suffering a skin affliction*) must be expelled from camp, until he is healed by God.

> ### *Maintain purity in the camp!*

Each zav (*one suffering from a bodily discharge*) and all those contaminated by contact with a corpse must also undergo ritual purification or face the prospect of karet (*being cut off*, cf. Lev. 15:31).

Offenses against God's holiness (such as swearing falsely, or making God a partner to a crime against another) can compound crimes against humanity (Num 5:6). A person who swears falsely must make verbal confession to right the wrong against God and man (Num. 5:7a).

Reparation must follow, including payment of an asham (*reparation*). If neither the wronged nor his kinsman redeemer is available to receive restitution, the guilty shall restore payment to the LORD by giving to the priest.

? *Study Num. 5:1-4. Milgrom [p. 34] comments that only here in this passage of Torah can deliberate sins against God be reduced by confession to inadvertent or unintentional sins, expiable by sacrifice. Do you agree? Explain.*

Vows and Blessing

> ❝ ADONAI said to Moshe, "Tell the people of Isra'el, 'If a man's wife goes astray and is unfaithful to him ... he is to bring his wife to the cohen ...'" ❞
>
> —Numbers 5:11, 15a

Zeal for marriage includes giving the jealous husband an opportunity to bring his wife before the LORD to check on her faithfulness (Num. 5:15). If cleared, she will be blessed with a better pregnancy (Num. 5:28). With no reciprocity, feminists charge that Torah unfairly singles out women. On the other hand, Talmud says the rite (including priestly interrogation and rough treatment of women) was never practiced.

More familiar passages in this segment about faithfulness and keeping close to the LORD include the Nazirite vow and the Aaronic benediction (Num. 6:1-21, 22-27). Putting on God's name reaps blessing!

Maintain purity of heart for your marital partner.

Brown [p. 161] applies the passage to Yisra'el, as God's mystic but erring bride. The prophets support her (Ez. 23:30-35), with connections to the curses of the covenant (Dt. 28:18, 37, 41). The immortal words cry out, HA'AZINU (*give ear!*, Dt. 32:1, 21), quoted by Paul (Ro. 10:19-20).

?• *Yisra'el has made vows to new husbands (whoring after gods of other nations). But God, her husband, has heard her vows and voided them at once! He's mercifully willing to take her back [Brown, p. 171]. Do you agree? Explain.*

The Tabernacle Sanctified

❝ On the day Moshe finished putting up the tabernacle, he anointed and consecrated it, all its furnishings, and the altar with its utensils . . . ❞

—*Numbers 7:1*

Note that the date of this section is one month earlier than the date of Num. 1:1 (cf. Ex. 40:2)! These supplementary materials detail the gifts made by each tribe, leader by leader.

All tribes help to inaugurate the tabernacle.

The order of the tribes for camping and marching (Num. 2) corresponds to the order for presenting gifts (Num. 7). The grandeur of the longest set of verses sets the stage for a magnificent dedication ceremony (Num. 7:1-89).

The leaders present a total of six wagons, fully equipped for transport of the tabernacle and its furnishings. The LORD instructs Moshe to give these wagons to the Levite clans of Gershon and M'rari, la'avod et avodat Ohel Mo'ed (*to serve the service of the Tent of Meeting*, Num. 7:5).

Each nasi (*exalted leader*) stands over the accounting to present a collective offering (Num. 7:2-3). Every day, in an identical procedure stressing consensual unity among tribes, one chieftain comes and presents the gift according to the command of God (Num. 7:11).

Read Num. 7:12. Explain why the tribes are led by Y'hudah. Explain why the segment cuts off after 5 days of offerings and concludes with the gifts of the sons of Shim'on. Why elevate Gad in the next segment? (cf. Gen. 49:19)

All Leaders Participate

❝ On the sixth day was Elyasaf the son of De'u'el, leader of the descendants of Gad. He offered . . . ❞

—Numbers 7:42-43a

The same n'si'im (*exalted leaders*), chosen to lead (Num. 1:5-16) and issue orders to encamp (Num. 2:3-31), are now called upon to give the gifts (Num. 7:12-83).

Once again, Gad fills the slot vacated by Levi in the order of the tribes (Num. 1:20-46; 26:5-62): R'uven, Shim'on, Gad; Y'hudah, Yissakhar, Z'vulun; Efrayim, M'nasheh, Binyamin; and Dan, Asher, Naftali. Once again, camps consist of two Leah groups, a Rachel group, and a concubines group—not the expected birth order.

Nasi derives from nasa (*to lift up*), the root of the present parashah name. The n'si'ei matot avotam (*exalted ones of their fathers' tribes*) have been elevated to head their respective clans or alfei Yisra'el (*the thousands of Israel*, cf. Jd. 6:12).

Exalt the exalted ones.

These same leaders will be called upon once more, when marching orders are issued and the LORD says it's time to move out (Num. 10:14-27).

? *Each day, a different nasi brings gifts from his respective tribe. How many days are gifts offered? Do you suppose that these are successive days? Explain why this might present a problem. Could you translate b'yom "when?"*

Identical Offerings

> ❝ On the eleventh day was Pag'i'el the son of 'Okhran, leader of the descendants of Asher. He offered . . . ❞
>
> —Numbers 7:72-73a

The n'si'im bring identical offerings, which include six covered carts and twelve oxen to present at the tabernacle. The wagons and oxen are apportioned with two wagons and four oxen for the Gershonites and four wagons and eight oxen for the Merarites.

Twelve days, twelve offerings, from twelve tribes.

The extreme repetition (Num. 7:10-88) derives from the legal language of an archival account. In each case, the gift begins and ends with the name of the nasi. In each case, the gift begins with mention of a silver dish, a silver bowl, and a golden spoon—all weighed in shekels and all filled with ingredients for a minchah, fine flour mixed with oil and incense. And in each case, the n'si'im donate the same number of bulls, rams, lambs, and goats.

The exact wording assures the reader that each tribe plays an identical role. Thus, no tribe monopolizes; every tribe is needed. Support comes from the tribes themselves, not from the Kohanim or L'vi'im.

? • Initiation of the altar follows consecration and purification. Read Num. 7:1-3, 10-12. Comment on the likelihood that the gifts for the altar were given through Passover, as in 2-18 Nisan (excluding Shabbats and convocation days).

The Voice of God

❝ When Moshe went into the tent of meeting in order to speak with ADONAI, he heard the voice speaking to him from above the ark-cover . . . from between the two k'ruvim . . . ❞   —Numbers 7:89

Sinai, where the people watched Moshe ascend the mountain to speak with the LORD (Ex. 24:16), now becomes an everyday possibility at the Ohel Mo'ed (*Tent of Meeting*).

God converses aloud!

High above the altar of incense, behind the curtain, in the Holy of Holies, above the ark cover that seals the decalog within the ark of the covenant, and between the k'ruvim (*cherubim*) . . . ADONAI calls out audibly to Moshe!

vaYishma et-haKol (*and he [Moses] listened to the Voice*, Num. 7:89). Rashi comments that the Voice was heard only by Moshe and not by the rest of the nation.

Commenting on Lev. 1:1, VAYIKRA el-Moshe (*and He called to Moshe*), Talmud asks why God prefaced "speaking" with "calling" [Yoma 4b]. The answer comes back that God spoke more loudly than with regular speech [Tos. haRosh.]. Others respond that the call to Moshe could be heard by all Yisra'el, but that the content of God's message was audible only to Moshe [Yoma 4b].

Study Ex. 25:22, Num. 7:89. What promise is fulfilled? Notice that Moshe enters the Tent of Meeting l'daber ito (to speak with Him). More than "speaking to," this implies "conversing/conferring with." Explain the difference.

Shimshon
Elevates the Nation

Meander

❝ *The woman bore a son and called him Shimshon. . . . ADONAI blessed him. The Spirit of ADONAI began to stir him when he was in the Camp of Dan, between Tzor'ah and Eshta'ol.* ❞ —Judges 13:24-25

Strength often impresses mankind. Samson's very name, derived from shemesh (*sun*), recalls the power of the celestial being who announced his birth and then disappeared in an ascending flame (Jd. 13:3, 20).

Nazirites vow to be close to God.

Shimshon's mother follows the angel's instructions. Once barren, she now carries the burden of her child's lifelong Nazirite vow. She avoids grapes, grape products, and unkosher foods (Jd. 13:4-5, 13-14). Her obedience is rewarded, when she births Yisra'el's strongest and most powerful man ever! Shimshon grows to become a mighty judge, who brings Yisra'el a measure of rest from the Philistines.

Final rest from the Philistine foe awaits David, who will slay their greatest warrior, Goliath. Shimshon, however, falls short. His lust for women ultimately leads to his downfall. He allows a Philistine woman to shave his hair, thus breaking his Nazirite vow and cutting off his power to save.

? *Study Jd. 13:25. Notice that Eshta'ol, Shimshon's stomping grounds, is not only close to Tzor'ah, but also to the major Philistine city of Gaza. Comment on the fact that Gaza, to this day, is inhabited by people named the P'lishtim.*

> ❝ While you have the light, put your trust in the light, so that you may become people of light. ❞
>
> —*John 12:36a*

Yeshua tells the crowd, ". . . as for me, when I am lifted up from the earth, I will draw everyone to myself" (Jn. 12:32). The claim extends beyond accepting shame and humiliation of death on a cross to save sinful men [Morris, p. 452].

In fact, God the Father elevates Yeshua to the very throne of heaven itself (Ps. 89:37; Mt. 26:64). In this way, Yeshua's "lifting up" conjoins his death and exaltation in a single word [Beasley-Murray, p. 215].

The crowd that listens is keenly aware that Yeshua has raised El'azar (*Lazarus*) from the dead (Jn. 12:17-18). Now Yeshua says, "If someone is serving me, let him follow me; wherever I am, my servant will be there too. My Father will honor anyone who serves me" (Jn. 12:26).

Walking in the light means acting on saving faith.

Yeshua closes this speech by urging those listening to act on the light that they have (Jn. 12:35). He urges those in the crowd to believe so that they become sons of light!

? *Read Heb. 10:21-22 and cf. Jn. 12:23-26. The one who gives his life to Yeshua becomes his servant. Explain how believers who "die to self" are spiritually elevated to the heavenly throne and assigned to Yeshua as Kohen Gadol.*

Talk Your Walk . . .

God commands Moshe, NASO (*elevate!*) the L'vi'im. Each clan—previously K'hat, now Gershon and M'rari—is lifted up to perform special tasks. Those of age get counted again and assigned to assist the holy kohanim in serving the nation. They purify the camp, set up and consecrate the tabernacle, receive offerings from each tribe, and dedicate the altar. Then, Moshe enters and hears the voice of God!

> *God elevates those who draw near to Him.*

In the Haftarah reading, Shimshon's supernatural birth to a barren woman is prophesied by an angel. The woman is commanded to avoid grapes and wine, and her son's hair must remain uncut for life. In return for fidelity to his Nazirite vow, Shimshon receives supernatural strength that delivers the nation from its Philistine foes.

In the B'rit Chadashah reading, anyone elevating Yeshua as Lord must remain strictly faithful to the covenant. Even as Yeshua gives his life and is subsequently exalted to the right hand of God, so now those who believe in Him must give their lives to become His servants. God elevated Yisra'el among nations when its priests, Levites, and judges stayed holy to their commitments; now those who elevate Yeshua are also lifted up!

Oasis

. . . Walk Your Talk

D o you walk in the light? Walking in the light is not difficult for one whose conscience is sensitive to God's Spirit. Those who choose to walk in darkness, Scripture says, choose to become slaves to the demands of the flesh (Ro. 6:15-19).

There's no getting around the need to exercise discipline. The priests and L'vi'im avoided unkosher foods and maintained ritual purity on those days when they entered God's holy place to serve on behalf of the nation. Shimshon, for all his lusts, maintained the oddity of uncut hair, showing clearly that he had been set apart to serve the living God. Has the LORD called you to the rigors of a disciplined life? Remember, the fruits of the Spirit include self-control.

But walking in the light goes beyond self control. Walking in the light requires you to abide in a spiritually pure state that can involve dying to self in moment-to-moment ways. Perhaps someone intends to do you harm, but you must avoid angry words spoken in a fit of anguish and pain. Perhaps you want to feel comfortable,

> *To live in God's Presence, abide in God's light.*

but God calls you into service. Are you motivated to comfort the flesh or stay on call to the LORD?

Shabbat Shalom!

בהעלתך
(B'-<u>HA</u>-A-LO-T'-<u>CHA</u>)
the lamps,
remember the Levites
shine light in the camps.
When you see the cloud lift,
move out and take Gramps.
Signal battle with trumpets,
then trample those tramps!

ADONAI will help you
win the war.
You won't complain
'bout quail no more.
You'll stop your thinkin'
that Moshe's a bore.
You'll respect your leaders,
and haShem you'll adore.

Walk B'HA'ALOT'CHA!
8:1-12:16

בְּהַעֲלֹתְךָ

In your making go up

TORAH—Numbers 8:1-12:16
- 1st Light the Night!—Numbers 8:1-2
- 2nd Dedicate the Levites!—Numbers 8:15
- 3rd Celebrate Freedom!—Numbers 9:1
- 4th Follow the Cloud!—Numbers 9:15
- 5th The Cloud Lifts!—Numbers 10:11-12a
- 6th Follow the Ark!—Numbers 10:35
- 7th Disorder in the Camp—Numbers 11:30-31
- Maftir Hung Up by Sin—Numbers 12:15-16

HAFTARAH—Zechariah 2:10(14-תִּנֵּי)-4:7
- Grace Supplied—Zechariah 4:7

B'RIT CHADASHAH—Revelation 11:1-19
- Lift Off to Heaven!—Revelation 11:19

In Your Making Go Up the Lamps,
Stay in the Light

➠ Looking Back

B'Midbar (*in the wilderness of*) Sinai, God says to number the earthly army of the LORD of Hosts. In His inner circle, He surrounds His dwelling with priests and their assistants, to safeguard it from encroachment by those not ritually pure. The rest of the house of Yisra'el encamps wherever assigned in the second protective circle, each tribe under its own respective banner.

> **B'Midbar** *Sinai, count all*
> *who can serve* **Adonai**
> *in His army and tabernacle.*
>
> **Naso!** *Raise up each clan*
> *to serve in its own special way.*
> *Each leader brings gifts*
> *to dedicate the altar.*
> *Above the mercy seat, God speaks!*
>
> *Tell Aharon:*
> **B'Ha'alot'cha** *et ha-nerot,*
> *in your making the lamps to go up,*
> *focus them to shine brightly.*

Following the pattern established at Mt. Sinai, God speaks to Moshe. Moshe then passes on God's instruction to Aharon and his sons and, in turn, to all the sons of Yisra'el encamped at the foot of the mountain. Eventually, the heritage passes on to us, as we continue wandering in the wilderness . . .

Naso (*elevate!*) everyone to holy service, God says, starting with the clans of Levi. Division of labor among the clans results in higher status tasks for the sons of K'hat and lower status duties for the sons of M'rari. By mentioning Gershon first in the new portion, attention is shifted to elevate all sons to glorious activity without kindling the jealousies of sibling rivalry.

L o g

In spite of different head counts and duties, each tribe brings exactly the same offering to dedicate the altar, enumerated in detail twelve times! Once completed, the LORD speaks, but only to the innermost circle of one! As at Sinai, Moshe ascends alone to hear the voice of the LORD.

Moshe receives instruction to tell Aharon: B'HA'ALOT'CHA et ha-nerot (*in your making go up the lamps*), focus them to shine brightly! Kohanim must stay awake nights to tend the fire. As they stay in the light, they abide in the Holy Place under the protection of the Holy One of Yisra'el.

Levites dedicated, Passover kept, trumpets blown, the camp moves out to follow ADONAI! Soon, however, the kvetching starts . . .

In B'HA'ALOT'CHA . . .

The Key People are Moshe (*Moses*), Aharon (*Aaron*) and sons, Levites, tribes and leaders, Chovav (*Hobab/Jethro*), the rabble, 70 elders, Eldad, Meidad (*Medad*), Y'hoshua (*Joshua*), Miryam (*Miriam*), and Moshe's Cushite/Ethiopian wife.

The Scenes include wilderness of Sinai and Paran, Tav'erah (*Taberah/"burning"*), Kivrot-haTa'avah (*Kibroth Hattaavah/ "graves of craving"*), & Chatserot (*Hazerot*).

Main Events include guide for lighting lamps and observing Passover; cloud/fire pillar to guide journey; trumpet signals; 1st move after 2+ years; "Kuma, ADONAI" (*Arise, O LORD*); complaints about manna, 70 elders to help Moshe; quail and plague; Miryam and Aharon speaking against Moshe; ADONAI confirming Moshe's authority peh el-peh (*mouth to mouth*); Miryam cast out 7 days; and camp moving.

The Trail Ahead ➡

The Path

וידבר יהוה אל משה לאמר
דבר אל אהרן ואמרת אליו
בהעלתך את הנרות
אל מול פני המנורה
יאירו שבעת הנרות

—במדבר ח/א-ב

ךְ	תְ	ל	עֵ	הַ	בְּ
letter: chaf sofeet	tav	lahmed	ayin	hay	bet
sound: **CHah**	T'	Lo	(silent)-ah	Hah	B'

in your making go up = B'HA'ALOT'CHA = בהעלתך

Work

The Legend

And spoke the Lord	va-y'daber ADONAI	וַיְדַבֵּר יְהֹוָה
to Moses, saying,	el-Moshe lemor	אֶל־מֹשֶׁה לֵּאמֹר׃
"Speak to Aaron	daber el-Aharon	דַּבֵּר אֶל־אַהֲרֹן
and you will say to him,	v'amarta elav	וְאָמַרְתָּ אֵלָיו
'In your making go up	b'ha'alot'cha	בְּהַעֲלֹתְךָ
→ the lamps	et-ha-nerot	אֶת־הַנֵּרֹת
toward the area (at the)	el-mool	אֶל־מוּל
face of the menorah,	p'nei ha-m'norah	פְּנֵי הַמְּנוֹרָה
will give light	ya'iru	יָאִירוּ
the seven lamps.'"	shiv'at ha-nerot	שִׁבְעַת הַנֵּרוֹת׃

—*Numbers 8:1-2*

Related Words

to go up, ascend, climb, immigrate, surpass	alah	עָלָה
going up (to Jerusalem, bema), immigration; immigrant	aliyah; oleh	עֲלִיָּה; עוֹלֶה
to be burnt, go up in flames; burnt offering	alah ba-esh; olah	עָלָה בָּאֵשׁ; עוֹלָה
the Most High, God, supreme, exalted, lofty, high	Elyon	עֶלְיוֹן
superman	ha-adam ha-elyon	הָאָדָם הָעֶלְיוֹן
attic (go up to the roof)	aliyat gag	עֲלִיַּת גַּג
to fluctuate, see-saw, go up and down	alah v'yarad	עָלָה וְיָרַד
genius	ilooyoot	עִלּוּיוּת

Hit the Trail!

Light the Night!

> **❝ ADONAI said to Moshe, "Tell Aharon, 'When you set up the lamps, the seven lamps are to cast their light forward, in front of the menorah.'" ❞**
>
> **—Numbers 8:1-2**

B'HA'ALOT'CHA et ha-nerot (*in your making go up the lamps*) . . . So begins this week's portion, as God gives instructions for Moshe to pass on to Aharon, the High Priest.

Tend the light throughout the night.

With the tabernacle complete (Ex. 40), priests ordained (Lev. 8), offerings received and the altar dedicated (Num. 7), the time has arrived for the mobile priesthood to tend the light that shines in the darkness (cf. Jn. 1:4-5).

Beyond tending the light through the night, the sons of Yisra'el make aliyah (*ascend* or *go up*) to the Promise Land. Spiritually, aliyah is ascending to the Presence of El Elyon (*God the Most High*).

Thus, the Levites "cause to ascend" the lamps (Lev. 24:2; Num. 8:2); the LORD "causes to ascend" His people from Egypt to the Promise Land (1 Sam. 8:8); the LORD "causes to ascend" Eliyahu when He takes him in a whirlwind (2 Ki. 2:1); and Shlomo "causes to ascend" the ark when he brings it up to the temple in Y'rushalayim (2 Chr. 5:2).

? *Ezekiel prophesies that the LORD will "cause to ascend" Israel from its graves (Ez. 37:13); but upon Tyre, God will "cause to ascend" the deep—it will be destroyed forever (Ez. 26:19). Describe how God "causes to ascend" His glory.*

Dedicate the Levites!

" After that, the L'vi'im will enter and do the service of the tent of meeting. You will cleanse them and offer them as a wave offering . . . "

—Numbers 8:15

Qualifying the L'vi'im for the avodah (*service*) of the tabernacle requires an involved ritual. First, they are sprinkled with the water of chatta't (*decontamination*); then shaved and bathed; last, their clothing is scrubbed (Num. 8:7, 11-12, 21).

> **The L'vi'im protect the sanctuary against encroachment.**

Thereafter, the ritual continues, with Yisra'el identifying with the L'vi'im by means of s'michah (*laying on of hands*, Num. 8:10).

Following purification, L'vi'im undergo dedication by being t'nufah lifnei ADONAI (*elevated before the LORD*), i.e. formally assigned to the LORD at the tabernacle and then given over to the service of the kohanim [Fox, p. 696, n11; Milgrom, p. 63, n13, 16].

Now subordinated to the kohanim, the L'vi'im are qualified for service (Num. 8: 11, 15, 21-22). In their new capacity, the L'vi'im become "lightning rods." In the event of encroachment by the sons of Yisra'el, God holds the Levites responsible for the offense.

Review Num. 8:19. Explain how the L'vi'im "effect-ransom" for the sons of Yisra'el [Fox, p. 697]. Why would God direct ketsef (wrath) at the on-duty Levite, rather than upon the son of Yisra'el who encroaches the holy things?

Celebrate Freedom!

> ❝ *ADONAI spoke to Moshe in the Sinai Desert in the first month of the second year after they had left . . . Egypt; he said, "Let the people of Isra'el observe Pesach at its designated time."* ❞ —*Numbers 9:1*

Exactly one year after the sons of Yisra'el depart Egypt, the day before the full moon on 14 Nisan, the sons of Yisra'el commemorate Passover (Num. 9:2-5).

Celebrate Passover, at the Tabernacle, at its appointed time.

Some, however, cannot eat the paschal lamb, because they are barred as a result of corpse contamination (Num. 9:6). The tam'u (*ritually impure ones*) consult Moshe, who then consults the LORD. God responds for this and subsequent times, saying that those who are either tamei or unable to celebrate as a result of being on a long journey can celebrate Passover exactly one month later, on 14 Iyar. All others must celebrate Passover at the prescribed, holy time or face karet (*being cut off*).

Torah does not specify whether God will take action to shorten one's life, cut off one's children or one's name; or even take away one's share, inheritance, or place in the world to come. However, each person bears his own sin. The same statute applies for both the ger (*stranger*) and the native alike (Num. 9:14).

> **?** *Read Lev. 7:20-21, then 1 Cor. 11:27-30. Describe the relationship in Torah between ritual impurity, eating the lamb, and karet (being cut off). Are believers being cut off in 1 Cor. 11:30? Explain. What does this mean for you today?*

Follow the Cloud!

> ❝ *On the day the tabernacle was put up, the cloud covered the tabernacle, that is, the tent of the testimony; and in the evening, over the tabernacle was what appeared to be fire . . .* ❞ —*Numbers 9:15*

Seven times, Torah states that the LORD alone directs and guides His people (note the use of al pi ADONAI, *according to the mouth of the LORD*, in Num. 9:18a, 18b, 20a, 20b, 23a, 23b, 23c). Milgrom [p. xxxi] observes that septenary references strongly emphasize the point being made. Thus, God answers Moshe's intercessory request to lead Yisra'el to the Land (Ex.33:14-17; *Walk Exodus!*, p. 162).

A variation of the portion name is subsequently used: Oo-l'fi <u>he'alot</u> he'anan (*whenever the cloud <u>lifted up</u>*) from the Tent, Yisra'el would journey on, and where the cloud settled, Yisra'el would encamp (Num. 9:17-18). Thus Yisra'el prepares to journey through the wilderness to the Land.

When the cloud lifts, the journey begins!

Sounding silver trumpets alerts the camp (Num. 10:1-10). Long blasts signal an assembly, and short blasts order the divisions to move out or go to war. The honeymoon journey into the wilderness is set to begin!

? Considering that the sons of Yisra'el do not leave Sinai until the next segment, there has been no movement or journeying since Exodus 19! Study Num. 9:17-20. Explain how these four verses describe a honeymoon experience.

The Cloud Lifts!

❝ On the twentieth day of the second month of the second year, the cloud was taken up from over the tabernacle of the testimony; and the people of Isra'el moved out in stages . . . ❞ —Num. 10:11-12a

Newlyweds spend a year together before going to war (Dt. 24:5); so Yisra'el also remains at Sinai for nearly 12 months. Suddenly the cloud lifts, and Yisra'el pulls up stakes. Finally, the journey through the wilderness begins!

Journey on up to the Land!

In the usual formation, Y'hudah and the eastern flank depart first, followed by M'rari and Gershon (Num. 2:1-3; 10:14, 17). R'uven and the southern flank journey next, followed by the sons of K'hat (Num. 10:21) carrying the ark. Behind the ark, Binyamin leads the western flank, followed by Dan and the northern flank.

When the cloud would rest, Y'hudah would stop first. Then the sons of Gershon and M'rari would erect the framework in advance of the next flank's arrival. Once prepared, they could receive the ark at the center of camp from the sons of K'hat [Baraita, D'melechet ha Mishkan, 13, cited in Ramban, Num. 10:17].

Study Ex. 40:38 and Num. 10:34. Comment on how both verses describe the nature of a journey from Mount Sinai to the Promised Land, a journey that has yet to begin! Why is scripture so vicarious about this journey?

Follow the Ark!

> **❝ When the ark moved forward, Moshe said, "Arise, ADONAI! May your enemies be scattered! Let those who hate you flee before you!" ❞**
> —*Numbers 10:35*

God's people sing Numbers 10:35 in the liturgy (*va-y'hi binsoa ha-aron . . . Kuma, ADONAI . . .*), as the scroll is lifted from the ark to circle amidst the people in a glorious event called the Torah Processional.

Starting in Numbers 2:17, Rav Bachya counts fifty paragraph spaces in the scroll culminating in Numbers 10:35-36. Y'hudah haNasi (*Judah, the Leader*, compiler of the Mishnah) calls this final paragraph a separate book of Torah [Shabb. 115a]. Inverted nuns (*n* for nikudot/*dotted*, also 50) set off this two-verse "book," a mini-Torah traversing the wilderness within the Torah.

Arise, O LORD!

Every Shabbat, the scroll is carried on the shoulders of living stones. Yisra'el, called B'MIDBAR (*in the wilderness of*) Sinai, is commanded: NASO (*elevate!*), surround, and guard the Torah. B'HA'ALOT'CHA (*in your causing to go up*) the light of Torah, God will "cause to ascend" His cloud to lead His people to the Promised Land! So we continue dor l'dor (*generation to generation*).

> **?** *Notice 50 spaces in Num. 2:17-10:35 on a scroll or Tikkun and the inverted "nuns" setting off Num. 10:35-36. Relate Num. 2:17 to Num. 10:35 (see p. 18). What happens after Num. 10:36? Explain why this phase could begin a new "book."*

Disorder in the Camp

❝ Moshe and the leaders of Isra'el went back into the camp; and ADONAI sent out a wind which brought quails from across the sea . . . covering the ground to a depth of three feet. ❞ —Num. 11:30-31

Quail blanket the ground three feet deep for a day's journey in every direction [Saadia, LXX, in ORT]. Each person gathers more than 300 gallons or a little over 1000 pounds of quail [ORT, Num. 11:31].

The ruach (*wind*) miraculously delivers these quail to a complaining people who ravenously demand meat at a site soon to be named Kivrot-haTa'avah (*graves of craving*). With the "meat still between their teeth . . . they buried the people who had-the-craving" (Fox, Num. 11:33a, 34b). Thus, the anger of the LORD flares against those who despise His provision of manna and demand meat instead.

Bury the greedy!

The Ruach "rushes upon" seventy elders, who prophesy but then stop (Num. 11:25). Then the "rushing Ruach" falls upon Eldad and Meidad (whose names signify "beloved of God," [Fox, p. 717, n. 26]); and they prophesy continuously (Num. 11:26). Now the ruach "rushes" quail to the camp—but this time, for judgment!

Read Num. 11:25-34. When the Spirit falls, the results can be for winnowing the wheat or separating out the chaff. Comment on how God's Ruach brings edification for some, judgment for others.

Hung Up by Sin

❝ *Miryam was shut out of the camp seven days, and the people did not travel . . . Afterwards, the people went on from Hatzerot and camped in the Pa'ran Desert.* ❞
       —Numbers 12:15-16

Moshe's lack of jealousy, when ADONAI puts His Ruach on Eldad and Meidad, contrasts sharply with his siblings' words: "Is it true that ADONAI has spoken only with Moshe? Hasn't he spoken with us too?" (Num. 12:2, cf. 11:29).

A jealous prophet cannot be elevated.

The LORD intervenes to protect His glory and maintain order in the camp. Moshe's prophesy is of a higher order, because he speaks with ADONAI peh el-peh (*mouth to mouth*, Num. 12:8). Communication occurs in the Holy of Holies, an elevated place only Moshe can access (Num. 7:89; 12:8).

Aharon repents and urges Moshe to intercede, because the LORD has stricken Miryam with tsara'at (*skin affliction*). Miryam must be expelled as tam'ah (*ritually impure*). Moshe intercedes, and the LORD heals her! But Miryam is defiled, rebuked, and shamed publicly, as if spat upon by her father (Lev. 15:8; Dt. 25:9). God orders her quarantined outside the camp, for seven days (Lev. 13:4; Num. 12:15).

?• *Review Num. 12:1. Explain why Miryam is singled out and not Miryam and Aharon. Read Lev. 13:4. Given that a human father's rebuke lasts seven days, comment on God's standard for rebuking Miryam. Why delay the march?*

Grace Supplied — *Meander*

> ❝ *What are you, you big mountain? Before Z'rubavel you will become a plain; and he will put the capstone in place, as everyone shouts, "It's beautiful! Beautiful!"* ❞
> —Zechariah 4:7

God comes to Tsiyon! Nil'vu goyim rabim el ADONAI . . . v'hayu li l'am (*many nations shall "be Levi" to the* LORD *. . . and become My people*; Zech. 2:10-11(14-15נ״צ)) on that day.

Thy kingdom come!

The journey begun in the wilderness ends at the temple. Kohen Gadol Y'hoshua is made pure—cleansed of the sin that caused destruction and exile (Zech. 3:4). He is commanded to walk with the LORD and await the LORD's servant, Tsemach (*branch*). Not by might, nor by power, but by God's Spirit shall the work be accomplished (Zech. 4:6). The m'norah—no longer requiring the vigilance of priests to shine through the night—receives an unending supply of olive oil straight from the olive trees of the Land!

All nations acknowledge the exalted role of Yisra'el among the nations. God levels the mount to make room for a special gift of grace. All will behold the temple on the mount, shouting, "Chen! Chen! (*Grace! Grace!*, Zech. 4:7)."

?• *Read Zech. 4:1-7. Relate the miracle of Chanukkah to Z'charyah's vision that the m'norah will never run out of olive oil. Explain the role of God's grace in building His temple and exalting Y'rushalayim among the nations.*

...ings / Lift Off to Heaven!

> ❝ Then the Temple of God in heaven was opened, and the Ark of the Covenant was seen in his Temple; and . . . flashes of lightning, voices, . . . thunder, an earthquake and violent hail. ❞ —Rev. 11:19

What begins with the chastising of Y'rushalayim (Rev. 11:1-2), and the mission of the two witnesses (Rev. 11:3-12), culminates in the rescue of the remnant (Rev. 11:13).

Heaven connects with earth!

Judgment begins on earth (Rev. 11:14-18), and the temple of God in heaven opens to the eyes of those on earth (Rev. 11:19). The ark of the covenant becomes visible in a Sinai kind of experience witnessed by all!

Miracles leap from the text! The two witnesses have power to shut up the skies, causing famine for three and a half years (Rev. 11:3). This event comes as the nations have power to trample the outer court for the same time period (Rev. 11:2). The witnesses are slain and lay unburied for three and a half days; but then they are raised to life and raptured to heaven, in the full view of those who celebrated and reveled in their deaths (Rev. 11:11-13).

The stage is set for the spiritual journey to culminate with heaven coming to earth!

? Read Rev. 11:19. Explain the significance that the ark of the covenant can be seen in the midst of the temple in heaven. Relate this event to the journey of the ark through the wilderness to the place where God will dwell.

Talk Your Walk . . .

T he journey to the Land finally begins! Kohanim tend the light throughout the night and protect the holy sanctuary from encroachment by the unholy. The nation follows God's cloud moving through the wilderness. The ark moves forward and covers three days in one! But disorder in the camp, greed for meat over manna, and slander even from Moshe's own sister, all conspire to hang up progress and bog down the nation.

In the Haftarah, miraculous progress resumes. The golden m'norah now connects directly to olive trees planted in the Land. No longer dependent on priestly perfection, the light shines continuously through the darkness.

A holy walk means seeing miracles on the way.

With God's grace at work, Yisra'el has finally become a light that shines continuously through the darkness.

In the B'rit Chadashah, what could not be seen even by Kohathites now can be seen by many! The holy ark of the covenant in heaven is visible from earth. What starts as chastening for Y'rushalayim becomes chastening for all the earth. Two olive trees become persons, holy witnesses with the power of Moshe in Egypt to inflict plagues on their enemies. The witnesses bring a drought for 3.5 years; then they lie slain for 3.5 days. God resurrects and raises them to heaven, paving the way to establish heaven on earth.

Oasis

. . . Walk Your Talk

arashat B'HA'ALOT'CHA describes the pattern for *ascending*. Yisra'el, called to national fellowship with the LORD, must set up lamps and face their light with seven-fold brilliance to enlighten the chamber of the Holy Place—a place of fresh challah and priestly fellowship with the LORD. We relive this memory every Shabbat when we light candles, drink wine, and break challah seasoned with salt—the time of kiddush (*sanctifying* the meal in fellowship with LORD).

The ark *carried up* on shoulders to the Promise Land ("being caused to *aliyah* ") would have fulfilled the literal meaning of this week's portion name. Instead, there unfolds a pattern of speaking "with" and "against" the LORD. The ark is mired down in the wilderness, and progress halts. Eldad and Meidad prophesy, but Miryam and Aharon rebel.

Believers cannot gossip or slander and still expect to behold God's temple with the holy ark making its

Walk your talk, and finish the journey!

descent from heaven to earth. God calls us to join ourselves to His kingdom. How are *you* preparing for the coming of the Ark of the Covenant?

Shabbat Shalom!

שלח לך
means "send for yourself!"
Send scouts to spy
on the land.
Beware of giants
who control the sand,
and yet
on the other hand . . .

Your sorry generation
has disobeyed,
so now My judgment
cannot be swayed.
You'll die in the desert
with bodies decayed,
while youngsters wear tsitsit
with garments unfrayed.

Walk SH'LACH L'CHA!
13:1-15:41

שְׁלַח לְךָ

Send for yourself!

TORAH—Numbers 13:1-15:41

HAFTARAH—Joshua 2:1-24

B'RIT CHADASHAH—Hebrews 3:7-4:11

Send for Yourself
(and Don't Trust the LORD?!)

← Looking Back

B'MIDBAR (*in the wilderness of*) Sinai, God says to number the earthly army of ADONAI-Tsva'ot. The priestly nation arises as His inner circle, surrounding the tabernacle to safeguard it from encroachment by those not ritually pure. The rest of the tribes encamp in the next circle, each under its own respective banner.

Following the Mount Sinai pattern, God speaks to Moshe, who passes instruction to Aharon, his sons, and all Yisra'el. Eventually, the heritage passes on to us.

Lift up the nation, God says, and NASO (*elevate!*) everyone to holy service, starting with the clans of Levi. Division of labor results in higher status tasks for K'hat and lower status duties for M'rari. By mentioning Gershon first, attention is

given to elevate all sons to glorious activity without kindling the jealousies of sibling rivalry. The innermost circle is closed off to all! As at Sinai, only Moshe ascends to hear the voice of the LORD.

Count all who can serve ADONAI
B'MIDBAR Sinai.
Arrange their tents in the camp.

NASO the clans to serve,
assigning each a special task.
But all tribes bring identical gifts
to dedicate the altar.
Then God speaks!

B'HA'ALOT'CHA, in your making
go up the lamps, Aharon is told to
focus them to shine brightly.
Levites dedicated, Passover kept,
trumpets blown, the camp moves!
But soon the kvetching starts.

Twelve spies you may SH'LACH
L'CHA, send for yourself,
but fear of giants
can set you back . . .

Cumulative Summary

Log

B'HA'ALOT'CHA et ha-nerot (*in your making go up the lamps*), Aharon is told to focus them to shine brightly. Kohanim must abide in the light, keeping awake to tend the fire all night in the Holy Place. By day, the ark with the Word of the LORD rises up and leads the way to the Land in which God promises to make His name dwell.

Departing Sinai, trumpets blast and the journey begins! This movement is the first in the text since the middle of Sefer SH'MOT (*Exodus*), when the sons of Yisra'el first encamped at Sinai.

As Yisra'el prepares to enter the Land, God accedes to their request to appoint scouts: SH'LACH L'CHA (*send for yourself!*) spies to scout the Land. The danger, though, comes when they receive the report . . .

In SH'LACH L'CHA . . .

The Key People are Moshe (*Moses*); one spy from each tribe (Shammua, Shafat, Kalev, Igal, Hoshea/Y'hoshua, Palti, Gaddiel, Gaddi, Ammiel, S'tur, Nachbi, G'uel); Amalek, haChitti (*Hittites*), haY'vusi (*Jebusites*), haEmori (*Amorites*), haC'na'ani (*Canaanites*); N'filim (*Nephilim*); the community, Aharon; and a Shabbat woodgather.

The Scenes include the Desert of Paran, C'na'an (*Canaan*) from the Desert of Tsin (*Zin*) to R'chov (*Rehob*) by L'vo Chamat (*Lebo Hamath*), Chevron (*Hebron*), Valley of Eshcol, Kadesh, Tent of Meeting, and Chormah (*Hormah*).

Main Events include sending spies, a bad report, God's desire to destroy the nation, Moshe interceding; 40 year delay, changing minds too late, defeat; laws about offerings; a man stoned for gathering wood on Shabbat; and tsitsit to remind us to follow the LORD's commands.

The Trail Ahead ➡

The Path

וידבר יהוה אל משה לאמר

שלח לך אנשים ויתרו את ארץ כנען

אשר אני נתן לבני ישראל

איש אחד איש אחד למטה אבתיו

תשלחו כל נשיא בהם

—במדבר יב/א-ב

שֶׁ	לַ	ח	לְ	ךָ
letter:	shin	lahmed	chet	lahmed	chaf sofeet
sound:	SH'	Lah	CH	L'	**CHah**

send for yourself! = SH'LACH L'CHA = שלח לך

Work

The Legend

And spoke the LORD	*va-y'daber ADONAI*	וַיְדַבֵּר יְהֹוָה
to Moses, saying,	*el-Moshe lemor*	אֶל־מֹשֶׁה לֵּאמֹר:
"Send for yourself people	*sh'lach l'cha anashim*	שְׁלַח־לְךָ אֲנָשִׁים
and they will spy out	*v'yaturu*	וְיָתֻרוּ
→ the land of Canaan	*et-erets C'na'an*	אֶת־אֶרֶץ כְּנַעַן
that I am giving	*asher-Ani noten*	אֲשֶׁר־אֲנִי נֹתֵן
to the sons of Israel.	*li-v'nei Yisra'el*	לִבְנֵי יִשְׂרָאֵל
One man,	*eesh echad*	אִישׁ אֶחָד
one man	*eesh echad*	אִישׁ אֶחָד
per tribe of fathers-his	*l'mateh avotav*	לְמַטֵּה אֲבֹתָיו
you-all will send,	*tish'lachu*	תִּשְׁלָחוּ
every leader among them."	*kol nasee va-hem*	כֹּל נָשִׂיא בָהֶם:

—*Numbers 13:1-2*

Related Words

go forth, yourself!(Gen. 12:1)	*lech l'cha*	לֶךְ־לְךָ
and he sent (Gen. 32:3(4))	*vayishlach*	וַיִּשְׁלַח
when he let go (Ex. 13:17)	*b'shalach*	בְּשַׁלַּח
delegate, envoy, messenger, emissary, agent	*shaliach*	שָׁלִיחַ
treats sent on Purim	*shalach manot*	שַׁלַח מָנוֹת
Let my people go! (Ex. 7:16)	*shalach et ami*	שַׁלַּח אֶת עַמִּי
scapegoat (goat sent-off)	*sa'ir ha-mishta-lei-ach*	שָׂעִיר הַמִּשְׁתַּלֵּחַ

Hit the Trail!

Send Forth Your Spies

> ❝ ADONAI said to Moshe, "Send men on your behalf
> to reconnoiter the land of Kena'an . . . From each
> ancestral tribe send someone who is a leader in his
> tribe." ❞
>
> —Numbers 13:1-2

The land is "good," but the people insist on reconnoitering; so the LORD grants their request. Both the idea to spy out the land and the request for carrying it out, though, are pushed by the people (Dt. 1:21-23, cf. Dt. 5:23-27(20-24‏תן‎)). God will not choose the leaders by lot [Ramban]. In fact, all tribes appoint scouts without God's help, according to the imperative SH'LACH L'CHA (*send for yourself!*). Levi does not participate; the others select younger, elite scouts.

As Moshe sends out the twelve spies, he poses six questions for them to explore. Are people strong or weak? few or many? Is the land good or bad? fat or lean? Is it wooded? Are the cities tented or walled? (Num. 13:18-20).

Yisra'el's scouts slander the Land.

During this season when the first grapes ripen (Num. 13:20), the spies will find that the land indeed flows. Yet ten spies will shout down Kalev's good report, fearing y'lidei ha-Anak . . . min ha-N'filim (*descendants of the giant from the original Titans*, Num. 13:27-28, 33; cf. Gen. 6:4). Perhaps spying wasn't a good idea . . .

?• *Re-read Num. 13:1-2. Comment on the fact that a minyan of spies, representing ten tribes, suffer a failure of nerve and a lack of faith; whereas two witnesses (leaders representing Y'hudah and Efrayim) follow God.*

The Spies Ascend

❝ *They went up and reconnoitered the land from the Tzin Desert to Rechov near the entrance to Hamat.* **❞**

—*Numbers 13:21*

Vaya'alu (*and they went up*, Num. 13:21), the first *aliyah* to the Land. Kalev sees his Judean inheritance (Num. 14:24; Josh. 15:20); but first he must drive out the "giants" (Josh. 15:14) and personally put to the sword the three sons of Anak [Jd. 1:10; Sot. 34b].

Either go up . . . or go down!

Giants intimidate the spies, causing the majority to give out dibat ha'aretz (*a bad report of the Land*). According to the El Amarna Letters, four-teenth century C'na'an is an Egyptian province ruled by governors and princes. The spies journey as far as Hamat, a large city 160 miles north of C'na'an, located on the Orontes River (Num. 34:8). Before being conquered by Assyrians, Hamat is called Hatti, the Hittite Empire in Anatolia, now Turkey.

Thus, the Land is routinely squeezed between empires. It literally "devours its inhabitants" (Num. 13:32). Discussing the geopolitical realities between empires, the spies see themselves as mere chagavim (*locusts*, Num. 13:33).

? *Read Lev. 13:12-13. If skin affliction "sprouts" and the afflicted person turns snow-white all over his body, the priest declares him pure! Explain how this can't be describing contagious leprosy.*

Y'hoshua Says to Enter

> ❝ If ADONAI is pleased with us, then he will bring us into this land and give it to us—a land flowing with milk and honey. ❞
>
> —Numbers 14:8

The sages say the nation tests the LORD ten times [Av. 5:4; cf. Num. 14:22]:

Ten strikes and you're out!

- at the sea (Ex. 14:11)
- at Marah (Ex. 15:24)
- without food (Ex. 16:3)
- gathering manna (Ex. 16:20)
- manna on Shabbat (Ex. 16:27)
- at R'fidim (Ex. 17:2)
- golden calf (Ex. 32:4)
- murmuring (Num. 11:1)
- manna not tasty (Num. 11:4)
- believing the spies' evil report against the land [Num. 14, Arachin 15a].

In spite of this testing, Y'hoshua and Kalev claim if the LORD is with them, Yisra'el can eat the giants like bread (Num. 14:8-9)! After all, manna is ground in mills or beaten in a mortar (Num. 11:8); it also melts in the sun (Ex. 16:21). When Y'hoshua urges that the enemies of God will melt in fear, though, he's nearly stoned for his encouraging words. God steps in to rescue him (Num. 14:9-11).

Moshe intercedes to stop God from annihilating Yisra'el (Num. 14:11-19). In the end, an untrusting generation must die in the desert for failing to walk in faith (Num. 14:23, 29).

> ❓ A guiding principle in scripture is midot k'neged midot, or "measure for measure." Yisra'el watched the ten plagues harden Egypt for judgment. Now the fathers test God ten times. Discuss the idea: "ten strikes and you're out!"

A Generation Judged

❝ *ADONAI said to Moshe and Aharon, "How long am I to put up with this evil community who keep grumbling about me?"* **❞**

—*Numbers 14:26-27a*

God decrees: Chai Ani (*as I live*), "all those-of-you-counted (for battle)" (Fox, Num. 14:29) shall drop in this wilderness! God lifts up His hand in an oath to swear that the entire generation will perish—except Y'hoshua and Kalev, the only ones who did not grumble against God (Num. 14:30). Thus, entrance into the Land is postponed for another forty years!

Curiously, the taf (*young*), whom the people said would become plunder, will be first to enter the Land (Num. 14:31). In fact, as the old generation dies off, the young "shall graze in the wilderness for forty years" v'nas'u et-z'nute-ichem (*thus shall they bear your whoring*) (Fox, Num. 14:33).

God's oath seals the fate of a generation of fathers.

As a down payment on God's oath, immediately the minyan of scouts who slandered the Land perish before the LORD (Num. 14:37). Then the young are given specific instructions to follow when they enter into the Land (Num. 15:1-7).

? *Recall Gen. 5:5, 8, 11, 14, 17, 20, 27, 31. Each father "died" after bearing sons (cf. Gen. 11). Study Num. 14:31-33, cf. Lev. 16: 21-22, Mt. 23:32. Explain how the sons "roam" (run free in the wilderness), bearing the sins of the fathers.*

Offering Meal and Drink

❝ When you prepare a bull as a burnt offering, as a sacrifice to fulfill a special vow or as peace offerings for ADONAI, there is to be presented with the bull a grain offering . . . ❞   —Numbers 15:8-9a

Juxtaposed with news in the previous segment that the fathers must die off in the wilderness, this segment directs the children to offer meal and drink offerings once they enter the Promised Land.

God gives the younger generation laws for the Land.

Actually, the ben bakar (*son of the herd*, i.e. bull) is offered as an olah (*ascent)* or sh'lamim (*fellowship*), as in fulfillment of a vow [Num. 15:8; cf. WALK LEVITICUS!, p. 36].

These additional meal and drink offerings graduate in a series to correspond with the size of the animal. Three times the flour and twice the wine and oil accompany the largest offering (Num. 15:11).

These rules bind not only the next generation entering the Land, but also the ger (*resident sojourner*, Num. 15:15). Ashley [p. 281] lists several more regulations that treat the citizen and the ger equally (Ex. 12:19; Lev. 16:29-31; 17:8, 10-12, 15-16; 18:26; 20:2; 22:18-20; 24:16; Num. 9:14; 15:26, 30; 19:10-12; 35:15).

? ● After the fathers have died, God directs the young who were "grazing" to enter the Land and make offerings accompanied by additional meal and drink offerings. Relate to Ro. 12:1 and S'udat Adon (the Lord's Supper).

Offering Challah

❝ *ADONAI said to Moshe, ". . . When you enter the land where I am bringing you and eat bread produced in the land, you are to set aside a portion as a gift for ADONAI."* ❞   —*Numbers 15:17-19*

hallah (*a loaf*) is baked only after the first of the dough is "lifted off" as a t'rumah (*offering*) for the LORD. The dough goes to the kohanim, and a blessing accrues to the donor's house (Ez. 44:30).

A new law for living with blessing on the Land.

Reisheet (*first of*) refers to the foods *"first processed,"* such as threshed grain or dough. Reisheet must be distinguished from bikkurim, the *"first-ripe fruits"* from the crop.

The command anticipates the leap to an agrarian society upon entry into the Land. The younger generation must tithe reisheet arisoteichem challah (*first-processed of your dough, a round loaf*) as a t'rumah, just like grain gifts from the threshing floor (Num. 15:20). The wheat must be separated from the chaff before the firstfruits from the threshing floor can be accepted [Ter. 1:10].

In this way, the LORD blesses the households which harvest or process and then tithe firstfruits from the Land.

Read Num. 18:12-13 and Ez. 44:30. Note that challah is also given to the priest by a non-farmer out of the fruits of his labor. Explain how the blessing arising from the gift rests on the home, not upon the crop.

Atoning for Sins

> **❝ If an individual sins by mistake, he is to offer a female goat in its first year as a sin offering. The cohen will make atonement before ADONAI . . . ❞**
>
> —Numbers 15:27-28a

Sinning b'yad ramah (*with a high hand*) blasphemes the LORD and results in karet (*being cut off*). For brazen defiance, an individual or his soul may be cut off from life in the community (or from future life either through one's children, or in the world to come, or both) (Num. 15:27-31).

Such is the predicament of the man gathering sticks on Shabbat. Binding, cutting, and carrying, all instances of m'lachah (*assigned tasks*), are prohibited on Shabbat. If the individual is suitably warned yet persists, sinning b'yad ramah (Num. 15:32-36), the offense demands karet. But no one knows which action to take [Sifri, Rashi in Sanh. 78b], so the man is brought before Moshe who consults the LORD.

Death is an atonement that satisfies the law.

The LORD's decree comes swiftly: "the man is to be put-to-death, yes death, pelt him with stones, the entire community, outside the camp!" (Fox, Num. 15:35). Thus, the community carries out capital punishment for the first time.

❓ Why did Moshe consult God, since God had already decreed death to those who work on Shabbat (Ex. 31:14, 35:2)? Read Num. 15:30-31, 35-36. Explain whether the man was cut off by the community, by the LORD, or both.

The Road from Mitzrayim

" I am ADONAI your God, who brought you out of the land of Egypt in order to be your God. I am ADONAI your God. "

—Numbers 15:41

The command to wear tsitsit (*tassels*) immediately follows the story of a man who intentionally engages in proscribed labor on Shabbat and is subsequently stoned by the community.

Guard your eyes, the windows of the soul.

Yisra'el must look upon tsitsit (*tassel* of four doubled threads with five knots, one hanging from each corner of a four-cornered garment) and remember the commandments of the LORD. Tsitsiyot remind the individual to look heavenward, with his eyes and heart upon the LORD's mitsvot (*commandments*). Concludes Rashi, "The heart and eyes are the spies of the body . . . the eye sees, the heart covets, and the body commits the transgression" [Leibowitz, p. 177].

To remember goes beyond recalling to mind. It includes making "real in the present what was real in the past" [Ashley, p. 295]. Remembering and doing God's commandments reflects membership in a royal priesthood—the opposite of enslavement to one's senses and going one's own way (cf. Romans 6:12-14).

Meditate on Num. 15:38. The t'chelet (blue) matches the blue of the mishkan's curtains and the Kohen Gadol's cords and robe (cf. Ex. 26:4, 36:11; 28:28, 39:21, 28:37, 39:31; 28:31, 29:22). What is the significance of royal blue?

Enter the Land

> ❝ *"Truly ADONAI has handed over all the land to us," they told Y'hoshua. "Everyone in the land is terrified that we're coming."* ❞
>
> —Joshua 2:24

Invasion begins in the days of the Iron Age (1200 BCE). Y'hoshua redeems the sins of the fathers, who slandered the Land with a bad report, by sending two spies—quietly, not publicly [Radak, Josh. 2:1]. The two spies walk the same ground and issue the kind of report that Y'hoshua and Kalev gave nearly forty years before! (Josh. 2:23-24).

As they reconnoiter the Land, the spies encounter a prostitute named Rachav, who essentially has a Passover experience. Rachav harbors the spies and conceals them from the king who searches for them (Josh. 2:1-7). As the spies hide for three days, Rachav follows their command to put a red marker on her house and remain indoors (Josh. 2:18, 22).

Only the obedient can rest in the promises of God.

The walls of Y'recho will fall, but Rachav and those who remain in her house will survive. In fact, Rachav ascends to marry into Yisra'el. She becomes yet another matriarch to enter the line of the King of kings (Mt. 1:5).

? *As a prostitute and a foreigner, Rachav is a marginal figure even in Y'recho. Dwelling in the city walls, her very existence is marginal—perched on the boundary between being in and out. Explain how God redeems marginal figures.*

> ❝ *For the one who has entered God's rest has also rested from his own works, as God did from his. Therefore, ... enter ... so that no one will fall short because of ... disobedience.* ❞ —*Heb. 4:10-11*

Believers have failed to enter spiritual rest since the beginning of time. Adam failed; the fathers of the wilderness generation failed; Y'hoshua failed; even David fell short (Heb. 3:8-12; Ps. 95:7-11). The author of Hebrews chides believers in his generation, "Watch out, brothers ... today, so that none ... become hardened" (Heb. 3:12-13).

The thought continues into chapter four: "Therefore, let us be terrified of the possibility that, even though the promise of entering his rest remains, any one of you might be judged to have fallen short of it" (Heb. 4:1). Entering spiritual rest is foundational to being imitators of God (Gen. 2:2; Heb. 4:4-9).

Work doubly hard to rest easy!

The grand finale admonishes believers, spoudasomen (*let us make haste*) to enter God's rest (Heb. 4:11). On day six, God created animals and man; fathers in the wilderness collected double manna; and Yeshua died, entering God's rest, saying, "It is finished!"

> **?** *Read 2 Tim. 4:9, 1 Thess. 2:17, cf. Heb. 4:11. Locate each use of the Greek verb spoudazo (to make haste, be zealous, give diligence, make every effort). Explain how one prepares to enter God's rest. What about next week's work?*

Talk Your Walk . . .

Ⅰn this parashah, God tells Moshe to tell the people, SH'LACH L'CHA (*send for yourself!*) spies to scout the Land. The tribes appoint their own scouts, who speak collectively to slander the Land by reporting that it devours its inhabitants. Though Y'hoshua and Kalev say enter, the other spies and the rest of the people shout them down. For their lack of faith, God judges the older generation to wander the wilderness forty years and die there. He orders the younger ones to rest in their faith and to offer meal and drink offerings upon entering the Land.

The Haftarah describes how Y'hoshua redeems the actions of the spies. Instead of sending one spy from each tribe with public fanfare, Y'hoshua quietly sends just two spies after his own heart. The spies give the same positive assessment that Y'shoshua and Kalev had reported forty years before. They confirm that the inhabitants fear Yisra'el. No longer does the old guard see itself as grasshoppers confronting giants!

> *Run the race,*
> *then rest with God.*

Believers in the B'rit Chadashah are chided for hardening against the calling of God. As the nation once refused to enter the Land, now believers are sternly warned not to resist entering God's rest. Believers should "make haste" without delay. One cannot imitate God and follow after Him without resting from work as God rests from His.

Oasis

. . . Walk Your Talk

Trusting God sounds easy, but walking in that trust requires far more. Under Moshe, the nation believed that military conquest required skilled combatants, strategies, reconnoitering, intelligence information, and the like. Tradition insists that armies were not actually needed until Yisra'el sent in the spies. Faith requires only that you see yourself as a son of God, called to face giants without fear!

When Yisra'el faced Pharaoh at Pi haChirot (*the mouth of freedom*), she crossed over without firing a shot. A generation later, when she faced Sichon and Og, she took up arms but did not lose a man! Facing the giants of the Land calls for faith in one's walk.

Are you standing up to the giants in your life? Y'hoshua trusted that the spies' report would enable him to discern the right timing. He knew he was appointed to cross over, but he didn't know exactly when. Timing is controlled by God.

Who opened the deep at the Sea of Reeds? Who felled the walls at Y'recho? Perfect faith ensures right timing—both running and resting with God! In what ways are you facing the giants in your life? How do you gauge God's rhythm, His ways, and His time table?

> *Perfect faith ensures perfect timing.*

 **Shabbat Shalom!**

קֹרַח greeted
God's plan with scorn,
left out, tho a Kohathite
and firstborn!
So he launched a rebellion
to unseat the priests,
saying, "We ALL are priests,
don't treat us like beasts!"

But the ground opened wide,
and Korach's house fell!
Then fire consumed
rebel firstborns as well.
A plague broke out,
tens of thousands died,
'til Aaron offered incense
to turn the tide!

Walk KORACH!
16:1-18:32

כֹרַח
Korah (bald)

TORAH—Numbers 16:1-18:32
- 1st Korach Rebels—Numbers 16:1-2a
- 2nd Moshe Accused—Numbers 16:14
- 3rd God Defends—Numbers 16:20-21
- 4th Counter-Attack—Numbers 16:44-45 (17:9-10 תּל״ך)
- 5th Aharon Exalted—Numbers 17:1-3 (16-18 תּל״ך)
- 6th Worship Restored—Numbers 17:10 (25 תּל״ך)
- 7th Tithe to the Levites—Numbers 18:21
- Maftir Tribute Paid—Numbers 18:32

HAFTARAH—1 Samuel 11:14-12:22
- A Kingly Theocracy—1 Samuel 12:22

B'RIT CHADASHAH—Acts 5:1-11
- A Priestly Church—Acts 5:11

Levi's Bald Spot and Unholy Desire

← Looking Back

B'MIDBAR (*in the wilderness of*) Sinai, everyone is counted and assigned a campsite. God surrounds His Presence with priests and their assistants, then with the rest of the house of Yisra'el.

> **B'MIDBAR Sinai,**
> **the camp gets organized.**
> **NASO each clan to serve ADONAI**
> **its own special way.**
> **B'HA'ALOT'CHA the light, let it**
> **shine bright through the night.**
>
> **SH'LACH L'CHA spies**
> **to scout the Land, but beware of**
> **fearing giants rather than**
> **trusting God.**
> **Don't sink into jealousy**
> **like KORACH, either! Baldfaced**
> **rebellion brings judgment on all.**

NASO (*elevate!*) everyone to holy service, God says, starting with the clans of Levi. Each has a special task; but as at Sinai, only Moshe ascends to hear the voice of the LORD.

B'HA'ALOT'CHA et ha-nerot (*in your making go up the lamps*), Aharon is told to focus them to shine brightly. Kohanim stay awake nights to tend the fire in the Holy Place. By day, the ark with the Word of the LORD rises up! It leads the way to the Land, where God promises to make His name to dwell. Silver trumpets signal God's marching orders. Departing Sinai, the journey begins! Right away, complaints follow.

SH'LACH L'CHA (*send for yourself!*) spies to scout the Land, God relents, when the people express doubt. Returning spies give a bad report, though, petrifying the children of Yisra'el! Because they lack the faith to overcome giants with God's help, the older generation is destined to wander the wilderness for forty years and die outside the Land.

Log

The faithless cannot enter to inherit the promises of God! The younger generation, however, receives different instructions. They must bear the sins of their fathers, awaiting God's time to enter the Land.

Revolt! Led by KORACH (*Korah/bald*), a bypassed firstborn Kohathite, the disenfranchised rebel. When the leadership of Moshe and Aharon is tested, the LORD's anger consumes the rebels. Twelve staffs are collected. Aharon's staff is the only one that buds, thereby reinforcing his authority as Kohen Gadol (*High Priest*). Instructions about tithing punctuate the need to support God's chosen leaders as they serve Him alone.

In KORACH . . .

The Key People are Korach (*Korah*), Datan (*Dathan*), Aviram (*Abiram*), On; Moshe (*Moses*); 250 leaders of the congregation; Aharon (*Aaron*); El'azar (*Eleazar*); and haL'vi'im (*the Levites*).

The Scene is near entrance to the Tent of Meeting; last location mentioned, driven to Chormah (*Hormah/ "destruction"*).

Main Events include Korach's revolt; ground opening to swallow rebels and their households; 250 more followers with censers consumed by fire; El'azar hammering bronze censers into altar covering as a memorial; more complaints and a plague; twelve rods collected, Aharon's buds as a sign against rebels; Levites given for help in tabernacle service while outsiders forbidden to approach God; and tithes and offerings first consecrated to the LORD, the rest used to support the priests.

The Trail Ahead ➡

The Path

ויקח קרח

בן יצהר בן קהת בן לוי

ודתן ואבירם בני אליאב

ואון בן פלת בנו ראובן

ויקמו לפני משה

—במדבר יו/א-ב

ח	רַ	קֹ
letter: chet	reish	koof
sound: CH	Rah	**Ko**

Korah (bald) = **KORACH** = קֹרֹח

Work

The Legend

And/now took	*va-yikach*	וַיִּקַּח
Korah, son of Izhar,	*Korach ben-Yits'har*	קֹרַח בֶּן־יִצְהָר
son of Kohath, son of Levi;	*ben-K'hat ben-Levi*	בֶּן־קְהָת בֶּן־לֵוִי
and Dathan and Abiram,	*v'Datan va-Aviram*	וְדָתָן וַאֲבִירָם
sons of of Eliab	*b'nei Eliav*	בְּנֵי אֱלִיאָב
and On, son of Peleth,	*v'On ben-Pelet*	וְאוֹן בֶּן־פֶּלֶת
(all) sons of Reuben.	*b'nei R'uven*	בְּנֵי רְאוּבֵן׃
And they rose up	*va-yakumu*	וַיָּקֻמוּ
to the face of Moses.	*lifnei Moshe*	לִפְנֵי מֹשֶׁה

—Numbers 16:1-2a

Related Words

Korah	*Korach*	קֹרַח
(rebellious) like Korah and his faction (congregation)	*k'Korach va-adato*	כִּקֹרַח וַעֲדָתוֹ
ice, cold, frost	*kehrach*	קֶרַח
to make bald, shear, pluck, uproot, become bald	*karach*	קָרַח
bald spot, bare place, forest clearing	*karchah*	קָרְחָה
glacier, iceberg	*karchon*	קַרְחוֹן
bald, hairless; or ice-vendor	*karchan*	קַרְחָן

Hit the Trail!

Korach Rebels

❝ Now Korach the son of Yitz'har, the son of K'hat, the son of Levi, along with Datan and Aviram, the sons of Eli'av, and On, son of Pelet, descendants of Re'uven, took men and rebelled . . . ❞ —Num. 16:1-2a

Excluded from the office of kohanim and given an "inferior service" of the tabernacle, Korach rebels. Four rebellions paint a picture of chaos and disorder: Levites vs. Aharon, firstborns vs. Moshe, n'si'im (*tribal chiefs*) vs. Aharon, and the community vs. Moshe and Aharon.

The disenfranchised are not content with their lot.

Korach feels disenfranchised. Moshe and Aharon, his cousins from first-born Amram, lead the people and the priests. The position of head of the family should go to Korach, next in line and the eldest of K'hat's second son, Yitzhar. But Moshe appoints Elitsafan, firstborn of K'hat's youngest son Uzi'el, to leapfrog Korach and head the clan instead [Ex. 6:16-22; Num. 3:30, cf. 16:28; Rashi].

Korach complains bitterly. Rav-lachem (*too much to you!*), he tells Moshe and Aharon (Num. 16:3). Resenting their power, he asks, "Is it too little that you have brought us up from a land flowing with milk and honey to cause-our-death in the wilderness?" (Fox, Num. 16:13).

? Study Num. 16:9, 13. Both questions begin, ha-m'at (is it too little)? Comment on how Korach twists the words of Moshe to his own advantage. Discuss whether Korach has a valid point. Or is he a demagogue stirring up trouble?

Moshe Accused

> **&& You haven't at all brought us into a land flowing with milk and honey, and you haven't put us in possession of fields and vineyards . . . We won't come up! &&**
>
> **—Numbers 16:14**

Firstborns Datan, Aviram, and On protest Moshe's leadership over them, responding lo na'aleh (*we will not go up!*, Num. 16:12-14). Suddenly, Egypt "flows with milk and honey," and Moshe has taken Yisra'el out to the wilderness to die!

Moshe goes straight to God, urging Him not to accept any minchah (*tribute*) from the rebels; for Moshe has taken nothing from them, nor has he wronged them (Num. 16:15). Moshe proposes to Korach that each person bring his own fire pan and incense, to test the alleged proposition that if all are holy and all the congregation are kohanim, then all can draw near to God with incense (Num. 16:17). Eager to be priests, Korach and his assembly take the bait!

Rebels approach God with unauthorized fire.

The next day, 250 chieftains approach the face of ADONAI, bringing fire and incense to the door of the Ohel Mo'ed (Num. 16:18, cf. Lev. 10:1-2). vaYera k'vod-ADONAI el kol ha-edah! (*and appeared the Glory of God to all the congregation!*, Num. 16:19).

?• Study Ex. 29:37-46, cf. Num. 16:15. Led by Korach, a Levite firstborn, a group of 250 leaders seeks to offer incense at the door of the Tent of Meeting where God meets with the Sons of Yisra'el. Why shouldn't God accept their minchah?

God Defends

❝ ADONAI *said to Moshe and Aharon, "Separate yourselves from this assembly; I'm going to destroy them right now!"* **❞**

—*Numbers 16:20-21*

Wrath kindled, God speaks: hibad'lu . . . va'achaleh otam k'raga (*separate yourselves . . . and I will devour them in an instant!*, Num. 16:20). Moshe and Aharon intercede on their faces to save the community.

God responds: he'alu misaviv l'mishkan-Korach, Datan, va-Aviram (*go up from around the dwelling of Korah, Dathan, and Abiram*) (Num. 16:24), because this mishkan is going down!

Moshe orders the community to move away from the tents and touch nothing. As Datan, Aviram, and all their household stand at the tents,

tiftach ha'aretz et-piha va-tivla otam (*the earth opens her mouth and swallows them*)—men, women, children, and possessions (Num. 16:32).

The earth devours the enemies of the LORD.

Fox translates, "So they went down, they and all theirs, alive, into Sheol" (Num. 16:33; cf. 17:5, 26:10-11). Family and property extend the personality of the head of the house [Fox, p. 741], so collective retribution exacts punishment on all. Korach's rebel community must suffer karet (*being cut off*) from all Yisra'el.

? *Read Num. 16:35, cf. Lev. 10:1-2, Num. 16:39-40 (17:4-5תו״). Draw analogies between the punishment of the 250 and that of Nadav and Avihu. Explain how El'azar's authority rises as a result of both instances.*

Counter-Attack

❝ ADONAI *said to Moshe, "Get away from this assembly and I will destroy them at once!" But they fell on their faces.* ❞

—*Numbers 16:44-45(17:9-10תג"י)*

Collective encroachment also brings judgment upon all Yisra'el! Once more, God reiterates: heromu . . . va'achaleh otam k'raga (*move aside . . . and I will devour them in an instant!*) (Num. 16:45(17:10תג"י); cf. 16:21).

> *There's nothing so bad that it can't happen.*

This time God's wrath focuses on the entire camp, for allowing collective encroachment upon the sanctuary. A plague breaks out, destroying 14,700. As the totals mount exponentially, Moshe directs Aharon to offer incense to atone for the community. Moshe is very specific about authorizing Aharon to obtain divine fire from the altar (Num. 16:46(17:11תג"י)).

As Aharon offers incense to make expiation for the community, he stands between the dead and the living (Num. 16:48(17:13 תג"י)). This time, the correct use of incense with authorized fire checks the plague and assuages the wrath of God (Num. 16:50 (17:15תג"י)). In Aharon's finest moment as Kohen Gadol, he saves the community from ruinous annihilation!

> ? ● *The priest stands between the dead and the living, effecting atonement (Num. 16:48,50(17:13, 15תג"י)). Discuss the job of New Covenant kohanim to offer prayers for those who face being cut off from the world to come (Heb. 13:10-17).*

Aharon Exalted

❝ *Adonai said to Moshe, "...take ... staffs ... from each leader of a tribe, twelve staffs. Write each man's name on his staff; and write Aharon's name on the staff of Levi ..."* ❞ —*Num. 17:1-3(16-18תנ"ך)*

Kach matteh (*take a staff*) from each tribal chief, including Aharon, God tells Moshe, and inscribe the name of the nasi (*leader*) on each one (cf. Num. 1:5-15; 2:3-31; 7:12-83; 10:14-27). Though Aharon is the seed of Levi's <u>second</u> son K'hat, his name is inscribed on the staff.

> ### God elects Aharon's dynasty to bear fruit.

The test for the priesthood exalts one tribal leader to head all others. Each staff is placed lifnei ADONAI (*before the LORD,* i.e. before the ark of the testi-mony). The following day, the matteh of Aharon had "put-forth a sprouting-flower, it had blossomed a blossom, it had ripened almonds!" (Fox, Num. 17:23).

The leaders gather to inspect, identify, and recover their staffs (Num. 17:24). It is obvious to all that God has fulfilled His word to choose the priestly leader and to muzzle the mut-tering of Yisra'el against Aharon (Num. 17:20).

The challenge turns to consolidating Aharon's authority and preserving the memory that God has exalted Aharon for all time.

❓ *Read Gen. 38:15, 25, 1 Sam. 14:43; cf. Gen. 49:10, Num. 21:18. Is the matteh of this segment a walking stick or the official staff of office? How does this understanding suggest the superiority of the Aharonic priesthood?*

Worship Restored

> *" . . . Return Aharon's staff to its place in front of the testimony. It is to be kept there as a sign to the rebels, so that they will stop grumbling against me and thus not die. "* —*Numbers 17:10(25תנ״ך)*

Place Aharon's staff as an ot (*sign*) to the rebellious that Aharon and his sons can approach the ark, while others face the danger of karev (*encroachment*) (Num. 1:51; 3:1; 10, 38; 18:7). The people get the message and react with great fear, saying, "Anyone who comes-near, comes-near (at all) to the Dwelling of YHWH will die" (Fox, Num. 17:28).

To stem the fears of the people, an agreement is reached and communicated to Aharon. From now on, L'vi'im will function as sacral guards bearing personal responsibility for lay encroachment. The sacral guards divert divine wrath from the community (Num. 1:53; 8:19; 18:1, 5).

Elevate L'vi'im to guard against lay encroachment.

Thus, the L'vi'im are entrusted with mishmeret (*military guard duty*). Tis'u et-avon ha-mikdash (*they shall bear the sin of the sanctuary*) in the event of lay encroachment (Num. 18:1). Now the laity can worship at the sanctuary, without fear of bringing divine wrath down upon themselves.

> *Read Num. 18:1, 8, 20. Only here and one other verse (Lev. 10:8) does the LORD give instructions directly to Aharon. Explain why God would choose this time to give Aharon a personal revelation.*

Tithe to the Levites

> 66 *To the descendants of Levi I have given the entire tenth of the produce collected in Isra'el. It is their inheritance in payment for the service they render in the tent of meeting.* 99 —Numbers 18:21

Mortal risks of guarding the Tent entitle the L'vi'im to additional rewards. God speaks to Aharon directly: I give over all ma'aser (*tithe, tenth*) to L'vi'im in exchange for their avodat Ohel Mo'ed (*service of the Tent of Meeting*) (Num. 18:21).

Pay the L'vi'im for taking risks for the nation.

Only the L'vi'im incur punishment in the event that someone encroaches upon the holy places of God [Milgrom, p. 155; Num. 18:23]. This regu-lation allays Yisra'el's fears of triggering another killer plague arising from encroach-ment (Num. 17:12-13(27-28 תג"ך)). Worship without fear at God's sanctuary is restored.

The L'vi'im inherit the tithes as t'rumot (*contributions*) which must be "lifted off" or separated out to God. Within the tithe is the ma'aser min ha ma'aser (*tenth within the tenth*), a one percent quantity that must be set aside by L'vi'im as t'rumat ADONAI and given over by God to the kohanim, priests who are exempt from tithe.·

? *Read Num. 18:12, 20; cf. Lev. 6:26(19תג"ך), Dt. 14:23. The choice grain, wine, and oil are set aside as t'rumat* ● *ADONAI. Explain Ramban's comment [p. 193] concerning fellowship with God: "I am thy portion—eat at My table."*

Tribute Paid

> ❝ Moreover, because you will have set aside from it its best parts, you will not be committing any sin . . . for you are not to profane the holy things of the people of Isra'el, or you will die. ❞   —Num. 18:32

Ma'aser (*tithe*) from an offerer turns to sachar (*wages*) for the Levite, once he pays the t'rumat ADONAI (*contribution belonging to the LORD*) to the kohanim. Called ma'aser sheni (*second tithe, tithing on the tithe*), this Levite's tithe changes the status of kodshei Yisra'el (*the holy or sacred gifts of Israel*) to wages for services rendered. The t'rumah is no longer holy and can be eaten anywhere.

Failure to tithe can be very costly (Lev. 22:14-16)! Even Levites, if they fail to set aside their share of the sacred tithe, incur fines requiring monetary compensation for touching or eating sacred offerings in a state of ritual impurity. If the offense is deliberate, the offender can incur karet (*being cut off*), a capital offense punishable by God (Num. 18:32; cf. Lev. 10:1-2, Num. 16).

God provides, but He demands His fair share.

For t'rumot to be eaten elsewhere, L'vi'im must tithe their own share to the kohanim. Only the kohanim do not tithe. Their role is to complete others' payment of tribute by eating the offering in a holy place, in fellowship with God.

> **?** Read Num. 18:32. Milgrom [p. 157] distinguishes chillel (*profane*) from timmei (*pollute, render impure*). Profaning the holy sanctuary renders the holy profane, but pollution renders the holy impure. Explain which is more serious.

A Kingly Theocracy *Meander*

> **❝ For the sake of his great reputation, ADONAI will not abandon his people; because it has pleased ADONAI to make you a people for himself. ❞**
>
> —*1 Samuel 12:22*

Sh'mu'el, appoints Sha'ul to be Yisra'el's first king. The request of the people, seen as an act of hostility against God's authority, is granted anyway (1 Sam. 12:1).

Coronating a king to rule a godly nation.

The coronation of Sha'ul (1 Sam. 11:14-15), and Sh'mu'el's defense of himself (1 Sam. 12:1-5), is followed by a defense of God (1 Sam. 12:6-11), the offense of the people for desiring a king for ungodly reasons (1 Sam. 12:12-18), and finally with the people admitting their lack of faithfulness (1 Sam. 12:19-22).

Irony abounds! Sh'mu'el, Korach's seed [Stone, p. 1186; cf. Ex. 6:24, 1 Sam. 1:19-20], sides with God's interests by insisting on kings who serve Torah, safeguard national righteousness, and bear God's glory.

The Haftarah ends with the people fearing kolot (*voices*), unusual thunder from the heavens (1 Sam. 12:18). Sh'mu'el intercedes for the people, assuring them that God will not abandon His people (1 Sam. 12:22).

? *Study 1 Sam. 12:22. The text emphasizes the central idea that God is pleased to make you His people [Keil and Delitzsch, Vol. 2, p. 121]. Contrast this idea with Korach's idea that every man should be a priest unto himself.*

> **❝ As a result of this, great fear came over the whole Messianic community, and indeed over everyone who heard about it. ❞** —*Acts 5:11*

Chananyah (*Ananias/ God is gracious*) and Shappirah (*Sapphira/ Beautiful*) hold back some proceeds from house and lands they claim to donate to God.

Don't be halfhearted and claim to be wholehearted!

Their misappropriation incurs swift retribution. Shocked, Peter asks how Chananyah could initiate such a deceit (Ac. 5:3). Chananyah falls over dead! Great fear falls upon those gathered, while they cover and bury him

in summary fashion (Ac. 5:5). Three hours later, his wife enters the scene. She, too, lies in an attempt to cover up the deception. Peter condemns her, and she falls over dead.

The ekklesia (*church*) and even those on the fringes are shocked, as Shappirah is hastily buried beside her husband (Ac. 5:10-11).

Swift and unforgiving retribution from God once again bolsters the authority of a godly institution. The first use of the word "church" occurs as those gathered fear God!

Review Ac. 5:5, 11. How is fear of the LORD the beginning of wisdom? Deceit, stealing, misappropriation of property deemed sacred, and a vain desire for praise are offenses against God. But what offense is punishable by death?

Talk Your Walk . . .

In this parashah, KORACH rebels against the LORD's authority by arguing that all men are priests. In the showdown, Korach leads the disenfranchised firstborns to offer incense. As Nadav and Avihu once died for unauthorized encroachment, so now the firstborns die a similar death. Korach's mishkan is swallowed by the earth, and only Aharon's incense can stem the plague that afflicts the entire assembly. The parashah ends with Aharon's authority consolidated. Tithes to the L'vi'im assure laity can worship without fear of punishment for encroachment.

Rebellion consolidates priestly authority.

In the Haftarah, Korach's descendant, Sh'mu'el, accedes to the people's demand for a king to rule over them, but he rebukes the people for wrong motives. He insists that a monarchy in Yisra'el establish a kingly theocracy—the king serving God and obeying Torah, not dominated by self-interest and seeking personal glory. Thunderous skies are reminders of the nearness of God's wrath, and so the people fear!

The B'rit Chadashah tells of followers holding back part of their own mishkan, while claiming wholehearted dedication to God. Both husband and wife die and get buried immediately. Once again, the people, here the Jerusalem "church," fear greatly. It becomes clear that New Covenant kohanim also kindle God's wrath when they transgress His holiness.

Oasis

. . . Walk Your Talk

B elievers walk in the high privilege of offering
the incense of sacrificial praise to God (Heb.
13:15). It requires faith to praise God in the
midst of difficult and trying circumstances.

Like Nadav and Avihu, the disenfranchised firstborns sought to draw near to God with offerings of
incense. They paid dearly, with their lives! The copper
altar, the place in front of the Tent of Meeting where
God meets with the people, would thereafter stand as
a reminder of their offense. The copper plating of this
altar of olah was the very copper of the incense pans
last touched by those 250 rebellious firstborns,
scorched by God's wrath.

As New Covenant kohanim, you must never forget that you are the living sacrifices of a priestly
church (Ro. 12:1-2). Yet, scripture goes on to warn
believers "not to have exaggerated ideas about your
own importance" (Ro.
12:3). Do not become like
Korach! Rather, stick to
the knitting. Pray and
intercede for others, as a

> *Use your authority
> to burn incense to God.*

New Covenant priest who abides in the Presence of
the Holy One. Take a moment now to consider how
you can best serve and delight in God!

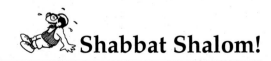 **Shabbat Shalom!**

חֻקַּת Torah
is a direct command
from the mouth of God
through Moshe's hand.
Take ashes of a cow
all rusty and tanned.
Mix with cedar and hyssop,
add water, let stand.

Sprinkle this mixture
to stop contamination,
'cuz touching the dead
defiles the nation.
Just speak to the Rock,
don't strike in vexation.
Keep God's statutes,
or die in desolation!

Walk CHUKAT!
19:1-22:1

חֻקַּת
Statute of

TORAH—Numbers 19:1-22:1

HAFTARAH—Judges 11:1-33

B'RIT CHADASHAH—John 3:1-21

Statutes Are
Simply Beyond Understanding

← Looking Back

B'MIDBAR (*in the wilderness of*) Sinai, Moshe counts the army, arranges the camp, and elevates Levites to guard the tabernacle from encroachment. Moshe is told, NASO (*elevate!*) special clans to pack and transport the tabernacle en route. All tribes dedicate the altar; then Moshe ascends alone to hear God speak!

B'HA'ALOT'CHA (*in your making go up*) the lamps, Yisra'el is instructed to light the m'norah and shine as a light to the nations. The cloud lifts, trumpets signal marching orders, and the journey begins! Kvetching is next.

If you can't trust God, SH'LACH L'CHA (*send for yourself!*) spies. But the report of giants in the land makes Yisra'el feel like grasshoppers! The faithless generation must die wandering.

Baldfaced rebellion follows! KORACH (*Korah/ bald*) assembles disenfranchised firstborns and displaced priests to set up his alternate priesthood. But God defends Moshe and Aharon, his chosen leaders. The ground swallows Korach's tent, along with the households of his rebel priesthood. Another 250 leaders get incinerated as they try to

B'MIDBAR *Sinai, number the army and organize the camp.*
NASO *Levites for special jobs.*
B'HA'ALOT'CHA *the lamps, let them shine brightly as you move out for God!*

Though spies SH'LACH L'CHA, *beware of fearing giants instead of trusting God. And don't sink into* KORACH's *rebellion! Accept the bald truth of your lot.*

The red cow purifies, if we follow the statute of instruction— CHUKAT *haTorah!*

Log

make holy smoke with their own censers.

The problem of corpse contamination arises in the aftermath of Korach's rebellion: this is CHUKAT (*the statute of*) instruction that ADONAI commanded . . . take a cow, red, flawless, without blemish . . .

God's mysterious ways unfold as Yisra'el obeys His statutes and cleanses the camp. Thirty-eight years pass, as a new generation grows up; but grumbling about food and water continues. Moshe snaps and strikes the rock. A second round of kvetching kindles God's wrath!

Poisonous vipers begin to bite and kill off more of the old guard. God tells Moshe to craft a bronze serpent and lift it up on a banner pole. To survive, the people must focus on the "lifted up" serpent.

In CHUKAT . . .

The Key People are Moshe (*Moses*), Aharon (*Aaron*), El'azar (*Eleazar*), Miryam (*Miriam*); kings of Edom, Arad, Amorites, and Bashan; and Yisra'el.

The Scenes include the Tent of Meeting, Midbar-Tsin (*Desert of Zin*), Kadesh, M'rivah (*Meribah*), Edom, Hor haHar (*Mt. Hor*), Negev, Chormah (*Hormah*), various stops on way to Mo'av, Yahtsah (*Jahaz*), Amorite territories and capital Cheshbon (*Heshbon*), Bashan, and Edrei.

Main Events include the statute of the red cow for purification; Miryam's death; Moshe striking the rock, which later bars his entry to the Land; detour around Edom; Aharon's death; more complaints, fiery serpent bites, and the bronze serpent lifted up; and more traveling, with defeats of Amorites and Bashan.

Yisra'el now marches on toward the Yarden . . .

The Trail Ahead ➡

The Path

וידבר יהוה אל משה ואל אהרן

לאמר זאת חקת התורה

אשר צוה יהוה לאמר

דבר אל בני ישראל

ויקחו אליך פרה אדמה תמימה

אשר אין בה מום

אשר לא עלה עליה על

—במדבר יט/א-ב

	ת	קַ	חֻ
letter:	tav	koof	chet
sound:	T	**Kkah**	Choo

statute of = CHUKAT = חקת

Work

The Legend

And spoke the LORD	*va-y'daber ADONAI*	וַיְדַבֵּר יְהֹוָה
to Moses and to Aaron,	*el-Moshe v'el-Aharon*	אֶל־מֹשֶׁה וְאֶל־אַהֲרֹן
saying,	*lemor*	לֵאמֹר:
"This (is the) statute of the Torah/instruction	*zot chukat ha-torah*	זֹאת חֻקַּת הַתּוֹרָה
that commanded the LORD,	*asher-tsivah ADONAI*	אֲשֶׁר־צִוָּה יְהֹוָה
saying,	*lemor*	לֵאמֹר
'Speak to the sons of Israel,	*daber el-b'nei Yisra'el*	דַּבֵּר אֶל־בְּנֵי יִשְׂרָאֵל
that they will take to you	*v'yik'chu eleicha*	וְיִקְחוּ אֵלֶיךָ
(a) cow, red, flawless,	*farah adumah t'mimah*	פָרָה אֲדֻמָּה תְּמִימָה
that isn't on her (a) blemish,	*asher ein-bahh moom*	אֲשֶׁר אֵין־בָּהּ מוּם
that (has)	*asher*	אֲשֶׁר
not gone up on her (a) yoke.'"	*lo-alah aleiha 'ol*	לֹא־עָלָה עָלֶיהָ עֹל:

—Numbers 19:1-2

Related Words

law, decree, statute, ordinance, rule, regulation, custom, boundary	*chok*	חֹק
constitution, law, custom	*chukah*	חֻקָּה
immutable law (ordinance forever)	*chukat olam*	חֻקַּת עוֹלָם
legal, lawful, licit/ illegal, unlawful, illicit	*chooki/lo-chooki*	חֻקִּי/לֹא־חֻקִּי
law-abiding (keeper of the law)	*shomer chok*	שׁוֹמֵר חֹק
international law (law among the peoples)	*chok ben-leumi*	חֹק בֵּין־לְאֻמִּי
military law (law of army/host)	*chok ts'vaee*	חֹק צְבָאִי

Hit the Trail!

Statutes for Defilement

" . . . the regulation from the Torah which ADONAI has commanded. Tell the people of Isra'el to bring you a young red female cow without fault or defect and which has never borne a yoke. " —Num. 19:1-2

Corpse contamination from the plague that killed 14,700 must be addressed. ADONAI commands, zot chukat hatorah (*this is the statute of the Torah/instruction*) for decontaminating individuals who have touched death.

Blood purifies by absorbing defilement.

The statute calls for taking a cow, at least three years old [M. Parah 1.1], to slaughter outside the camp under priestly supervision (Num. 19:3, 5). The parah adumah (*reddish cow*) must be completely red, without even two hairs that are not red [Par. 2:5]; without blemish (Lev. 22:18-22); and lo alah aleha 'ol (*never go up upon her a yoke*) (Num. 19:2)—in other words, the cow must never have worked in the secular sphere.

Outside the camp, the cow is slaughtered, and the blood is caught directly from the cow's neck [Sifri, Yad, Par. Adum. 4:4 in ORT]. Along with cedar, hyssop, and crimson wool, the entire cow is burned to ashes, including its skin, flesh, blood, and dung.

Read Lev. 5:6. Note that female offerings cleanse individuals, while the community and priests require a male offering. Now read Heb. 13:10-13, Num. 19:3. How can blood burned outside the camp, not at the altar, cleanse sins?

Sprinkle the Contaminated

> ❝ *A clean person is to take a bunch of oregano leaves, dip it in the water and sprinkle it on the tent, on all the containers, on the people who were there . . .* ❞
> —*Numbers 19:18*

An ish tahor (*clean person*) dips and sprinkles those being cleansed of corpse contamination. Paradoxically, he himself becomes tamei (*ritually impure*) in the process (Num. 19:19, cf. Lev. 16:22, 2 Cor. 5:21).

> ### *Sprinkling holy water absorbs the impurities of corpse contamination.*

Neither the one who slaughters nor the one who consecrates becomes tamei. It is the burnt blood which absorbs the impurity and then, through contact with the mei niddah (*waters of* separation*), renders the handlers tamei (Num.19:21). Only contact with the burnt blood of a cow that has been consecrated (set apart as holy) and then used for sprinkling renders the ish tahor tamei!

The segment continues with Miryam's death and burial by the whole congregation at Kadesh (note time frame, p. 179). Will Moshe and Aharon receive the grace accorded Kalev and Y'hoshua, or will they be the last of the old guard to die? The people gather to "assemble against" Moshe and Aharon one more time (Num. 20:2-5, cf. 16:3, 19).

> **?** *Read 2 Cor. 5:21. Note that the Greek translates, "For He made Him who knew no sin to be sin for us . . ." Explain how Yeshua became the sins of the world at the time of His death outside the camp. Relate to Heb. 10:5-14, Num. 19:8.*

Speak to the Rock

> **" . . . Take the staff, assemble the community, you and Aharon your brother; and before their eyes, tell the rock to produce its water. You will bring them water out of the rock . . . to drink. "** —Num. 20:7-8

Commands God: dibartem el ha-sela' (*speak to the rock*, Num. 20:8). Moshe and Aharon assemble the assembly before the boulder, and Moshe says: "Now hear, (you) rebels, from this boulder must we bring you out water?" (Fox, Num. 20:10). He strikes the boulder twice, and water gushes forth (cf. Ex. 17:6-7).

But disobedience triggers God's wrath! He responds: Ya'an lo he'e'mantem bi l'hakdisheni (*because you did not trust in Me to sanctify Me holy*), you shall not bring this assembly into the Land (Num. 20:12).

Moshe and Aharon disobey and get cut off.

Thus, Moshe and Aharon are doomed to die in the wilderness as the last of the fathers, the corporate heads of the generation cursed to die B'MIDBAR Sinai. The segment concludes, hemah mei m'rivah (*these are the Waters of Quarreling*) where the sons of Israel quarreled, va-yikadesh bam (*and He was sanctified through them*, Num. 20:13).

? *Compare and contrast parallel accounts of complaints for water in Ex. 17:1-7 and Num. 20:1-13. Explain why the next generation faces the same test as their fathers. Finally, what sin barred Moshe and Aharon from the Land?*

Send to Esav Your Brother

❝ Moshe sent messengers from Kadesh to the
king of Edom: "This is what your brother Isra'el
says: you know all the troubles we have gone
through . . ." ❞   —Numbers 20:14

VaYishlach...mal'achim
(*and he sent ahead . . .
messengers/angels*) to
his brother in Edom (Num.
20:14, cf. Gen. 25:30, 36:1, 8, 9,
especially Gen. 32:4-5). The
nation of Yisra'el follows the
footsteps of patriarch Ya'akov,
returning to the Land.

*Yisra'el extends chesed
to his brother, Esav.*

The messengers convey a
formal epistolary letter beginning, "You know..." [Milgrom,
p. 167, n.14]. A matured Esav
has become the "king" of
Edom, and once more Yisra'el
is greeted by the threat of
overwhelming force (Num.
20:20-21, cf. Gen. 32:4, 33:1).

Yisra'el requests permis-
sion to pass through and not
stray off the King's Highway
(Num. 20:17). They further
sweeten the deal by offering
to pay for drinking water
from the Zered River, a
financial boon to Edom
(Num. 20:19). But this
time, Esav does not
accept the offer of tribute from
Yisra'el [Num. 20:18, 20-21; cf.
Gen. 33:10-11, *Walk Genesis!*,
p. 145]. Thus, the negotiations
with Edom prove fruitless.

? Read God's injunction to Yisra'el in Dt. 2:4-5. Explain
how decisions made by the fathers impact the destiny of
● the sons, even hundreds of years later. Why does Yisra'el
tell Edom that the LORD, too, sent "an angel" (Num. 20:16)?

Continue the Priesthood

> ❝ They traveled on from Kadesh; and the people of Isra'el, the whole community, arrived at Mount Hor. ❞
>
> —Numbers 20:22

Aharon's death occurs atop Mount Hor (Num. 20:27-29). It is the first of Av in the fortieth year, after a lifetime of 123 years (Num. 33:38). Ordinarily, one sits shivah for seven days (Gen. 50:10; 1 Sam. 31:13); but in the case of Yosef's death, the community mourns for 70 days (Gen. 50:3), just short of the 72 days Egyptians mourn for Pharaoh [Von Rad, p. 425].

With the whole community watching, Moshe, Aharon, and El'azar ascend Mount Hor. El'azar returns, wearing Aharon's priestly garments (Num. 20:26). Kol ha-edah (*all the community*) weeps for thirty days in profound respect for the days of Aharon.

Aharon dies, but the high priesthood continues.

Ashley [p. 396] shows that an element of degradation or punishment is suggested by the imperative, hafshet (*strip!*) Aharon's garments (Num. 20:26), reminiscent of the stripping of Yosef's garments (Gen. 37:23). Moshe complies, and El'azar dons his father's vestments. The office of Kohen Gadol continues on.

?• Compare Num. 20:24, 27; Gen. 25:8, 17; 35:29; 49:33; Num. 27:13; and Dt. 32:50. After death, but before burial, a person ye'asef el ammav (is gathered to his kin). Look in 2 Sam 12:23 for a hint of an "afterlife in Sh'ol." Comment.

Walk through Desolation

> **" In response, ADONAI sent poisonous snakes . . .
> many of Isra'el's people died . . . The people of
> Isra'el traveled on and camped at Ovot. "**
>
> *—Numbers 21:6, 10*

This segment has mysterious beginnings. Stern starts at v.6 rather than v. 10. This more familiar passage tells of ha-n'chashim has-s'rafim (*the fiery serpents*) sent to bite the older generation, after they grumble once more about being led out to die in the wilderness (cf. Ex. 14:11).

Walk through the valley of the shadow of death.

Last time, Moshe told the people: hit'yats'vu oo-r'u et-y'shuat ADONAI (*stand fast and see the salvation/Yeshua of the* LORD) (Ex. 14:13).

This time, the LORD orders Moshe to make a serpent and lift it up so that the people may "fix their gaze upon" it and live (Num. 21:8-9). Later, the people will idolize this n'chash n'choshet (*bronze serpent*) and name it N'chushtan (2 Ki. 18:4). Still later, Yeshua will refer to this serpent as He tells Nicodemus how to receive eternal life (Jn. 3:14-16). The "lifting up" of the Son of Man will become the way of salvation for all who are condemned to die B'MIDBAR Sinai.

The march continues from Ovot to points beyond . . .

? *Year forty ushers in the last phase of the older generation condemned to die in the wilderness. Read Num. 21:17-18.*
• *What is the role of living water? Explain why Pisgah (Num. 21:20; Dt. 34:1) is the last stop in the wilderness trek.*

Offer Peace to the C'na'anim

> ❝ *Isra'el sent messengers to Sichon, king of the Emori, with this message: "Let me pass through your land. We won't turn aside . . ."* ❞
>
> —*Numbers 21:21-22a*

VaYishlach ... mal'achim (*and he sent ahead messengers*) to Sichon, the Amorite king. Moshe requests to follow the King's Highway, trying to reach the Yarden and cross into the Promise Land. As with Edom (Num. 20:14), Yisra'el offers peace (Dt. 2:26).

Offer peace first, but trust God for the victory.

Previously, Yisra'el followed a tortured path through uninhabitable wilderness in order to skirt lands held by relatives Edom, Mo'av, and 'Amon. When negotiations proved fruitless (Num. 20:21), God expressly commanded Yisra'el to show chesed (*covenant kindness*) to his brother Edom (Dt. 2:4-5).

In contrast, this time God commands Yisra'el to fight the Amorites when peace fails (Dt. 2:30-36). Earlier, Sichon had invaded Mo'av and seized his lands on the Yarden. But now, the poem describing Sichon's victory over Mo'av is quoted in the context of Yisra'el's victory (Num. 21:24-31). No mercy for Canaanites who won't accept peace!

❓ *Read Gen. 10:6, 15-17. Explain whether or not the Amorites are Canaanites. Read Dt. 2:26; 20:10. Explain why sending messengers and offering peace precedes holy wars. Read Dt. 2:30 and explain why God hardens hearts.*

Arrive at Mo'av

> **❝** *Then the people of Isra'el traveled on and camped in the plains of Mo'av beyond the Yarden River, opposite Yericho.* **❞**
>
> —*Numbers 22:1*

Once more, the journey (not the jihad) focuses the segment, this time the maftir. Following Yisra'el's awesome victories over Sichon and Og, the nation encamps in the area that overlooks its final entry into the Promised Land.

Last stop on the wilderness journey.

It should not go unnoticed that Moshe participates in a major victory over a Canaanite giant, considered stout as an oak and last of the giants of Refa'im, one who slept in a 13-foot bed (Am. 2:9; Dt. 3:11).

Now Yisra'el stops me'ever l'Yarden (*from across the Jordan*), overlooking Jericho (Num. 22:1). Sefer D'VARIM (*the Book of Deuteronomy/words*) commences in the same area, b'ever haYarden (*across the Jordan*, Dt. 1:1, 5). Here, Moshe gives his final oration before dying at Pisgah, overlooking the steppes of Mo'av. Forty years have passed. The rest of the Torah (Num. 22-Dt. 34) reports the events which occur on the banks of the Yarden, just prior to entering the Land.

? *Read Num. 25:1, 33:49. Name the last camping site of Yisra'el, prior to crossing into the Land. Note that all laws in Sefer D'VARIM are given on the steppes of the banks of the Yarden. Compare Num. 22:1 and 36:13; comment.*

> ❝ So Yiftach crossed over to fight the people of 'Amon, and ADONAI handed them over . . . it was a massacre. So the people of 'Amon were defeated before the people of Isra'el. ❞   —Judges 11:32-33

Despised because his mother is a prostitute and driven out by his siblings (Jd. 11:1-2), Yiftach (*Jephthah*) lives as an outcast in exile. But when his town Gil'ad (*Rugged Country*) becomes desperate, they offer him the judgeship to fight the invading Ammonites (Jd. 11:4).

Redeeming a bad situation.

Yiftach consents, only if the Gileadites make him rosh (*head*) after he succeeds (Jd. 11:9). Then begins a lengthy quote from Parashat CHUKAT, which recounts that this land of Gil'ad belongs to Yisra'el as a result of their victory over the Amorites (Jd. 11:19-22, Num. 21:21-25; cf. Dt. 3:16).

Yiftach offers peace to Ammon the aggressor, but negotiations fail (Jd. 11:27). Before the battle, Yiftach utters a rash vow (Jd. 11:30-31). Then he routs the Ammonites (Jd. 11:32-33).

The Haftarah passage ends abruptly, before Yiftach makes good on his vow. Thus, emphasis remains on the peace entreaty, negotiations, and ultimate victory.

? *Read Gen. 19:37-38, Dt. 2:9, Jd. 11:17, 32-33. Under what circumstances does Yisra'el war against his cousins, the Ammonites? When is war avoided? Read Jd. 11:35-36. Explain the daughter's willingness to honor her father's vow.*

> ❝ *But everyone who does what is true comes to the light, so that all may see that his actions are accomplished through God.* ❞
>
> — *John 3:21*

Nakdimon (*Nicodemus*) holds the office of teacher among the P'rushim (*Pharisees*), but can't grasp how being born again can relate to entering the kingdom of heaven (Jn. 3:4, 7, 12).

> *Trust that God sheds light on acts which glorify Him.*

Yeshua alludes to the bronze serpent being lifted up in the wilderness (Jn. 3:14, cf. Num. 21:9). Those who were bitten and dying were not saved because of the serpent, but because they were obedient to watch the bronze ser-

pent being lifted up. In like manner, those who are dying in the flesh are saved when they watch with eyes of faith the lifting up (death and resurrection) of the Son of Man.

God sheds light on acts which glorify Him (Mt. 5:16). La'asot emet (*to do the truth*) corresponds in Greek to poiein ten aletheian (*keep the faith*) [Barrett, p. 218; Brown, p. 135 on Jn. 3:21]. Thus, the ones who practice a life walk will come to the light and see the Son of Man being lifted up. Those who choose evil cannot see the truth.

> ❓ *Read 2 Ki. 18:4. Explain how fixing on the serpent degenerates into idolatry with time. Expand on the idea that lifting up the Son of Man also connotes a willingness to follow Him to the cross, so that he's lifted up in one's life.*

Talk Your Walk . . .

P arashat CHUKAT (*the portion "statute of"*) focuses on commandments that are not easily grasped by conventional thinking. Thus, the statute of the red cow to remove defilement from corpse contamination makes little sense from a medical point of view. But then, speaking to a rock shouldn't obtain water.

Statutes require faith that ventures beyond reason.

Nor should <u>lifting up</u> a bronze serpent save the bitten from dying. Nor should offering peace to enemies promote victory on the battle front.

The Haftarah reading reinforces exercising faith beyond reason, when Yiftach offers peace to the invading Ammonites. Negotiations with this cousin-nation fail, so Yiftach trusts the LORD for the victory. The Ruach rests on him as he battles to reclaim Gil'ad, previously conquered by Moshe. Yiftach makes a rash vow, however, which should have been annulled to avoid literal fulfillment.

In the B'rit Chadashah, the Son of Man says He must be "lifted up," much in the same way that Moshe "lifted up" the bronze serpent B'MIDBAR Sinai. In the wilderness, those who looked upon the risen serpent obeyed God's statute and lived. Even so, the B'rit Chadashah offers life only to those who are willing to "lift up" their lives on the execution stake with Messiah. "Lifting up" brings life to those who share in Messiah's sufferings!

O a s i s

. . . Walk Your Talk

To live a life that is spiritually pleasing to God may require you to sacrifice in ways that are simply beyond the ken of human understanding. It's not for you to decide how to do this! God will call you in His perfect time. Do not try to engineer your circumstances! The children of Yisra'el didn't have to go out looking for serpents. The serpents in life will come your way soon enough. The question is, what will you do about them when the biting starts?

Watch for the patterns of life. Sons and daughters grow to parenthood and then face the prospect of dying in the wilderness. The journey can be long and twisted. Are you a hopeful Y'hoshua or Kalev who lives out the hope-filled thoughts and perseveres to the end? You must be willing to face giants and look up from serpent bites. You must count it worthy to stand in God's light, even if the journey

> *Are you willing to walk with God in dangerous places?*

means walking in the valley of the shadow of death. You must not fear evil (Psalm 23:3-4) and know your anointing is what follows (Psalm 23:5). But you must first be willing to lift up the Son of Man, before He will lift you up!

 **Shabbat Shalom!**

When בלק watched
Sichon's defeat,
he freaked out first,
then ran to meet
Bil'am the curser
to avoid retreat.
He wanted victory,
Yisra'el to beat.

Even donkeys know
you need God's permission!
Despite Balak's finances
for this mission,
Bil'am couldn't curse us
with deadly precision.
So he uttered, "Mah Tovu,"
a blessed decision!

Walk BALAK!
22:2-25:9

בָּלָק

Balak (destroyer)

TORAH—Numbers 22:2-25:9
- 1st The Destroyer Reacts—Numbers 22:2
- 2nd Walking a Tightrope—Numbers 22:13
- 3rd A Fast Departure—Numbers 22:21
- 4th To the Summit—Numbers 22:39-40
- 5th To Moshe's Grave Site—Numbers 23:13
- 6th Mah Tovu—Numbers 23:27
- 7th A Pox on your House—Numbers 24:14
- Maftir Spear the Plague!—Numbers 25:9

HAFTARAH—Micah 5:7(6תִּנֵ״ך)-6:8
- Mah Tov—Micah 6:8

B'RIT CHADASHAH—Romans 11:25-32
- Covenant Love—Romans 11:32

Balak the Destroyer Fails to Destroy

◀ Looking Back

B'MIDBAR (*in the wilderness of*) Sinai, Moshe surrounds the tabernacle with tribes, each camping under its own banner. Levites fence off encroachment by unholiness. Moshe is told, NASO (*elevate!*) special clans to pack and carry the tabernacle. All tribes help dedicate the altar. Then God speaks!

B'HA'ALOT'CHA (*in your making go up*) the lamps, Yisra'el is instructed to light the m'norah and shine as a light to the nations. The cloud lifts, the trumpets sound, the journey begins!

If you must, SH'LACH L'CHA (*send for yourself!*) scouts to reconnoiter. But ten of the twelve spies report that this land is unconquerable. The people are so huge, they make Yisra'el feel like grasshoppers! Lack of faith brings a lifetime of wandering, kvetching . . .

. . . and revolt! KORACH (*Korah/ bald*), suffering the jealousy of sibling rivalry, gathers the disenfran-

> *Count everyone B'MIDBAR Sinai,*
> *and set up camp around God's Tent.*
> *NASO Levites for holy tasks,*
> *telling Aharon:*
> *B'HA'ALOT'CHA the lamps,*
> *shine brightly for God!*
>
> *Time to move out! If you must,*
> *SH'LACH L'CHA scouts up ahead.*
> *But don't fear the giants*
> *or rebel like KORACH!*
> *Accept the bald truth of your lot.*
>
> *If we follow CHUKAT haTorah,*
> *the red cow's ashes will purify.*
> *Yet even Moshe disobeys*
> *after so much whining!*
> *Lifting up the bronze serpent*
> *is the only way to save us.*
>
> *Though BALAK would destroy,*
> *God will bless us!*
> *"How lovely are your tents,*
> *O Ya'akov!"*

Log

chised and sets up his own alternate priesthood. God defends Moshe's authority, and the ground swallows the counterfeit mishkan! His anger consumes rebel firstborns, incinerated as they try to make holy smoke with their own censers. A budding staff indicates God's choice for Kohen Gadol—Aharon, Moshe's brother.

Death of the rebels brings with it the problem of corpse contamination. **CHUKAT** haTorah (*the statute of instruction*) concerning the red cow reveals how to cleanse the camp. God's ways are mysterious! Lifting up a bronze serpent to save lives confirms that!

Not convinced? When a donkey talks and curses turn to blessing, **BALAK** (*Balak/ destroyer*) discovers just how powerful the God of Yisra'el is . . .

In BALAK . . .

The Key People are Balak, messengers, Bil'am (*Balaam*), ziknei Mo'av v'Midyan (*elders of Moab and Midian*), the donkey, the angel, Amalekites, Kenites, Yisra'el (*Israel*), Moabite women, and Pinchas (*Phinehas*).

The Scenes are Mo'av (*Moab*), P'tor (*Pethor*), the Arnon border, Kiryat Chutsot (*Kiriath Huzoth*), Bamot Ba'al (*Bamoth Baal*), s'deh Tsofim al-rosh haPisgah (*field of Zophim on top of Pisgah*), rosh haP'or (*top of Peor*), and Shittim.

Main Events include Balak buying curses; Bil'am's donkey balking and talking; permission to speak only God's words; three high places visited, altars built; Bil'am blessing Yisra'el, saying *Ma tovu*, and prophesying enemies' destruction; Yisra'el joining with Moabite women and gods at covenant feast, even in the camp; plague; and Pinchas spearing couple to stop plague.

The Trail Ahead ➡️

The Path

ויָרְא בָּלָק בֶּן צִפּוֹר אֵת כָּל

אֲשֶׁר עָשָׂה יִשְׂרָאֵל לָאֱמֹרִי

וַיָּגָר מוֹאָב מִפְּנֵי הָעָם מְאֹד

כִּי רַב הוּא

וַיָּקָץ מוֹאָב מִפְּנֵי בְּנֵי יִשְׂרָאֵל

—בְּמִדְבַּר כ״ב/ב-ג.

קָ	לָ	בָּ
letter: koof	lahmed	bet
sound: K	**Lah**	Bah

Balak (destroyer) = **BALAK** = בָּלָק

Work

NaN## The Legend

And saw	*va-**yar***	וַיַּרְא
<u>Balak</u>, son of Zippor,	*<u>Balak</u> ben-Tsipor*	בָּלָק בֶּן־צִפּוֹר
→ all that did	*et kol-asher-asah*	אֵת כָּל־אֲשֶׁר־עָשָׂה
Israel	*Yisra'el*	יִשְׂרָאֵל׃
to the Amorites.	*la'Emori*	לָאֱמֹרִי
And feared Moab	*va-**yagar** Mo'av*	וַיָּגָר מוֹאָב
before the people greatly,	*mip'**nei** ha-**am** m'od*	מִפְּנֵי הָעָם מְאֹד
because many he (was),	*ki rav-**hoo***	כִּי רַב־הוּא
and (was) distressed Moab	*va-**yakats** Mo'av*	וַיָּקָץ מוֹאָב
before the sons of Israel.	*mip'**nei** b'**nei** Yisra'el*	מִפְּנֵי בְּנֵי יִשְׂרָאֵל׃

—*Numbers 22:2-3*

Related Words

Balak, king of Moab ("destroyer," "devastator")	*Balak*	בָּלָק
to destroy, lay waste	*balak*	בָּלַק
to destroy	*billek*	בִּלֵּק
to be destroyed	*boollak*	בֻּלַּק
to teach someone a 'lesson' (teach so-and-so a 'Balak')	*l'**lamed** et ploni 'Balak'*	לְלַמֵּד אֶת פְּלוֹנִי 'בָּלָק'

Hit the Trail!

The Destroyer Reacts

> ❝ Now Balak the son of Tzippor saw all that Isra'el had done to the Emori. ❞
>
> —Numbers 22:2

Reeling from the demise of Sichon and Og, the Moabites unite with Midianites. Mo'av had relied on Sichon and Og for protection [Rashi]. Balak, king of Mo'av, fears that as an ox uproots grass and leaves nothing underfoot, so Yisra'el will trample all surrounding tribes.

Balak, the destroyer, hires Bil'am to curse Yisra'el.

He hires Bil'am to curse Yisra'el. But as God had once intervened to protect the patriarchs from the wiles of Lavan (Gen. 31:24) and Avimelech (Gen. 20:3), so now God warns Bil'am: "You are not to go with [the nobles of Balak], you are not to curse the people, because they are blessed" (Num. 22:12)—blessed from the avot (*fathers*, Gen. 27:33).

Thus the gentile prophet, who knows the exact moment when blessing and cursing is most likely to occur, cannot press God to curse a people who enjoy blessings to the thousandth generation (Num. 22:6; Josh. 24:9-10; cf. Ex. 20:5-6). The covenant promised the patriarchs distinguishes Yisra'el among the nations!

Review Gen. 20:3, 31:24, and Num. 22:9. Each instance describes the way God "came to" someone who did not enjoy the raised-up status of a prophet. Explain how prophets are more elevated than those who dream.

Walking a Tightrope

> **❝ Bil'am got up in the morning and said to the princes of Balak, "Return to your own land, because ADONAI refuses to give me permission to go with you." ❞**
>
> **—Numbers 22:13**

Bil'am speaks God's words to the nobles, "... ADONAI refuses to give me permission to go with you" (Num. 22:13). Yet things change quickly in the Middle East! Balak sees this refusal to walk with his nobles as part of a negotiation process. He antes up by sending sarim rabim v'nichbadim me'eleh (*nobles, more of them and more honored than these*, Num. 22:15).

Bil'am walks a tightrope. On one hand, he downplays the issue of money, saying, "Even if Balak were to give me his palace filled with silver and gold ..." (Num. 22:18a).

On the other hand, Bil'am must steadfastly abide by the principle of speaking only what God says: "... I cannot go beyond the word of ADONAI my God to do anything, great or small" (Num. 22:18b).

Bil'am tries to obey God and still get paid, too.

That night, God reinforces Bil'am's duty—he can go with the second delegation, ach et ha-davar asher adaber eleicha oto ta'aseh (*but the word that I speak to you, that you will do!*, Num. 22:20).

? *Read Num. 22:18. Fox labels "great and small" a merism [p. 770], translating the phrase "anything at all." In your opinion, is Bil'am a cunning profiteer—or does he demonstrate integrity toward God, whom he calls "my God?"*

A Fast Departure

❝ *So Bil'am got up in the morning, saddled his donkey and went with the princes of Mo'av.* ❞

—*Numbers 22:21*

Saddling his own donkey at daybreak, Bil'am hastens to join the second delegation en route to cursing Yisra'el. Vayichar-af Elohim . . . l'satan lo (*and the nostrils of God flared . . . to "Satan" him*, Num. 22:22). The angel of the LORD blocks the road as an adversary to Bil'am's she-donkey!

Bil'am's speedy departure resembles Avraham's on the day God told him to journey to Moriah to offer his son, Yitzchak, as an olah (*ascent offering*). Avraham and Bil'am both saddle their own donkeys and depart at daybreak with two others (Gen. 22:3; cf. Num. 22:21-22). But Avraham hastens to seek God for blessing, whereas Bil'am hastens to seek God for cursing!

Bil'am hastens to do evil!

Three times, God's angel blocks the donkey's path. When Bil'am vents his own anger, God opens the donkey's mouth to speak! The segment ends with Bil'am once more vowing to speak only those words God gives him to say (Num. 22:38).

? *Commenting on Lev. 26:7, the midrash says, "This is the proper way, that is, that when a man of eminence goes out on a journey, two people should attend on him" [Num.R. 20:13]. Compare and contrast Avraham and Bil'am.*

To the Summit

" Bil'am went with Balak. When they arrived at Kiryat-Hutzot, Balak sacrificed cattle and sheep, then sent to Bil'am and the princes with him. "

—*Numbers 22:39-40*

Arriving at Kiryat Chutsot, the outer markets of the city's suburbs, Balak offers sacrifices. The next morning, Balak and Bil'am ascend Bamot Ba'al (*high places of Baal*). Here, atop Idol Hill, Bil'am can view the "edge" of the people he hopes to curse (Num. 22:41).

See and curse!

Seeing the victim empowers the one who curses [Milgrom, p. 193]. Bil'am separates himself from Balak to set the stage: ulai yikareh ADONAI likrati (*perhaps the LORD will chance to call me*, Num. 23:3).

The LORD, in fact, puts a word in Bil'am's mouth, in the same way that He speaks to Aharon (Ex. 4:15), Yirmiyahu (Jer. 1:9), and all subsequent prophets (Dt. 18:18). Thus, Bil'am receives official prophetic treatment by the LORD, during these times that he is pledged to say only those words which the LORD puts in his mouth (Num. 23:12, cf. 22:38; and also note Num. 23:26, 24:13).

? *Study Lev. 1:1. Milgrom [p. 195, n4] references the Midrash, which compares Moshe (whom God "calls to") with Bil'am (whom God "happens upon"). Compare/contrast vaYikra and vaYikar [hint: see Walk LEVITICUS, p. 16].*

To Moshe's Grave Site

> ❝ Balak said to him, "All right, come with me to another place where you can see them. You will see only some of them, not all; but you can curse them for me from there." ❞   —Numbers 23:13

Balak takes Bil'am to a second site near the peak of Pisgah, called Field of the Watchmen (Fox, Num. 23:14) or Lookout Field.

Bil'am blesses Y'hudah from Pisgah.

Perhaps a change of place will bring about a change of luck [RH 16b]. Exclaims Balak, "you will see only some . . . not all" (Num. 23:13). Balak fears that seeing " too many Israelites would once again turn his curse into a blessing" [Milgrom, p. 198, n13].

Bil'am leaves Balak with his last olah (*ascent offering*). He separates himself, in the event that yikar ADONAI el Bil'am (*the LORD happens upon Balaam*, Num. 23:16). In fact, God puts a word upon his mouth. Bil'am declares to Balak: Kum (*arise!*) . . . Ha'azinah (*give ear!*) . . . (Num. 23:18) . . . "Look, I am ordered to bless; when he blesses, I can't reverse it . . . Here is a people rising up like a lioness; like a lion he rears himself up" (Num. 23:20, 24a). Ya'akov's prophecy of blessing for Y'hudah (cf. Gen. 49:9) comes to light!

> ❓ Look at Dt. 34:1, cf. Num. 23:14. Comment on the mystery that both Moshe's future grave site and the second place Balak tries to curse Yisra'el are in the same region. Relate justice and mercy to the fact that God blesses Yisra'el.

Mah Tovu

❝ Balak said to Bil'am, "Come, I will take you now to another place; maybe it will please God for you to curse them for me from there." ❞

—Numbers 23:27

Balak moves to rosh haP'or (*the summit of Peor*), the place where sons of Yisra'el will consort with daughters of Midyan (Num. 23:28, cf. Num. 25:1-3). Va-t'hi alav Ruach Elohim (*and the Spirit of God was upon him*), and Bil'am exalts in the glories of true prophecy [Ramban; Num. 24:1-2].

What Bil'am meant for evil, God means for good.

Prophesying nofel oo-g'lui einayim (*fallen prostrate and with uncovered eyes*), Bil'am declares:

Mah Tovu (*how goodly*) are your tents, O Ya'akov; your dwellings, Yisra'el (Num. 24:5). Thus begin the prayers of the morning liturgy, with prophetic blessing from a gentile seer who fully realizes the impossibility of cursing those whom God blesses!

Bil'am concludes, "When they lie down they crouch like a lion or like a lioness-- who dares to rouse it? Blessed be all who bless you! Cursed be all who curse you!" (Num. 24:9). Thus ends the third blessing. Balak rages, and Bil'am speaks a fourth time (Num. 24:15-24).

? Bil'am attains prophetic status to utter a blessing which is still sung daily in the morning prayers of Jews throughout the world. Sing the song of Mah Tovu, and explain how this blessing impacts your faith.

A Pox on your House

❝ But now that I am going back to my own people, come, I will warn you what this people will do to your people in the acharit-hayamim. ❞

—*Numbers 24:14*

Bil'am's fourth blessing prophesies the coming of Messiah and the end of all surrounding hostile nations, including Mo'av, Shet, Edom, Se'ir, Amalek, and even Ashur (Assyria)! Bil'am and Balak go their separate ways.

Balak acts on Bil'am's evil counsel to destroy Jewish holiness, by enticing the sons of Yisra'el to commit harlotry at covenant feasts to Mo'av's most disgusting god, Ba'al-P'or (*lord of baring*). Anything goes at these covenant feasts. Reports Rashi [p. 243] on why the god was called P'or, "Because they <u>bared</u> their but-

tocks before it and relieved themselves—this is the way it was worshiped."

 ## Judgment!

God's wrath flares against Yisra'el; a plague erupts; and God orders Moshe: Kach . . . v'hoka otam la-ADONAI neged ha-shamesh (*take . . . and impale them before the LORD against the sun*, i.e. *publicly*; Num. 25:4). Stunned, the entire congregation weeps at the door of the Tent, just as a Simeonite prince and Midianite princess saunter by . . .

Note Ps. 30:5(6מוֹ) and Is. 26:20. Ber. 7a adds that God has a moment each day when He passes judgment, and only Bil'am knew that exact moment (Num. 24:16). Read Num. 23:8. Can Yisra'el ever be cursed? Explain.

Spear the Plague!

" . . . nevertheless, 24,000 died in the plague. "
                                        —Numbers 25:9

On duty, Pinchas grabs his spear and follows the couple el ha-kubbah (*into the innermost chamber/"womb"*) of the tent. As they lie together, Pinchas plunges his spear through both man and woman, el-kovotahh (*into her womb*, Num. 25:8). Says Rashi, "He struck precisely at Zimri's male organ and her female organ" [p. 346].

The plague God sent to consume the people stops instantly! Twenty-four thousand lie dead, slain by the wrath of God. But Pinchas, son of Puti, a Kohathite with a foreign-born mother, shows zeal for the covenant. His bravery stems the plague and assuages God's wrath.

Zeal's day in the sun!

Pinchas could have been tried for murder, despite the divine decree to impale offenders and put their heads on a pike in open daylight. Instead Pinchas son of Puti, long considered ineligible as Kohen Gadol (doubly so after being in a tent with the dead), will be exalted by God to the highest honor!

? Review the maftir. Explain how the shvi'i section could be summarized by the actions of Pinchas. Read Romans 11:26-27. How does the zeal of Pinchas compare with Messiah's coming as Go'el (kinsman redeemer)?

Mah Tov   *Meander*

❝ *Human being, you have already been told what is good, what Adonai demands of you—no more than to act justly, love grace and walk in purity with your God.* **❞**
                                              —Micah 6:8

Mah tov (*what is good*)? Hertz calls Micah 6:8 "the most important utterance in prophetic literature" [p. 683].

Ethical living must accompany sacrifice.

The question asks what is the way of true worship. Micah, a contemporary of Yesha'yahu (*Isaiah*) and first to predict the coming destruction of Y'rushalayim (Mic. 3:12), answers. With a rhetorical question, he makes the point that true worship requires more than cultic substitution for righteousness, with its olot (*ascent offerings*), rivers of oil, and even sacrificing firstborns to atone for sins (Mic. 6:6-7).

God makes His case against Yisra'el for breaking His covenant (Mic. 6:1-2). He will cut off the cities, sorceries, idols, and centers of idolatry (Mic. 5:10-13). Yisra'el must walk in purity or face judgment.

Most importantly, God demands three changes: to do mishpat (*justice*), love chesed (*covenant kindness*), and hat-snea lechet (*to walk modestly*) (Mic. 6:8).

? *Read Mic. 6:5; Micah recalls Balak's attempts to curse Yisra'el. Remember that Balak utters the third blessing beginning "Mah Tovu" at Shittim. Relate curses of the covenant to curses from enemies. Explain the differences.*

> **" For God has shut up all mankind together in disobedience, in order that he might show mercy to all. "**
>
> **—Romans 11:32**

Yisra'el's cumulative failings pile up sins, triggering God's wrath. Hardening and partial blindness result (Lev. 26:14-16; Dt. 28:65, 32:28-29; Is. 6:9-13).

In a response of sheer mercy, God pops the scales off the eyes of the elect (Ac. 9:18). And one day, after Rav Sha'ul finishes his work among the gentile nations, God promises to finish opening the eyes of "all Yisra'el!" (Ro. 11:7-8, 25).

God reveals a "mystery." All mankind has been justly imprisoned or "shut up" in disobedience so that God can reveal His chesed (*covenant kindness*) to Yisra'el: "Out of Tziyon will come the *Redeemer*, [go'el, cf. Is. 59:20] . . . and this will be my covenant with them, . . . when I take away their sins" (Ro. 11:26-27).

God demonstrates how justice and mercy work.

Until then, gentiles must not be "wise in their own eyes" (Ro. 11:25). Yisra'el's partial blindness blesses the gentiles first. God further states, "by your mercy" (Ro. 11:31), Yisra'el will be shown the same mercy which shifted salvation to the gentiles!

? Read 2 Cor. 7:8, 10-11 and Ro. 11:29. Both verses capture the Greek word ametameleytos (not-with-sorrow/regret), usually translated "irrevocable." Explain why God does "not regret" engineering a process that greatly curses Yisra'el.

Talk Your Walk . . .

In parashat BALAK, the Destroyer pays Bil'am to curse Yisra'el. But God protects Yisra'el from all curses hurled by sorcerers and enemies. On three occasions, Bil'am goes to high places to survey Yisra'el; but all God allows him to speak are words of blessing. The greatest seer of the gentiles, Bil'am, is blinded to God's angel, yet saved from destruction, only because God opens the mouth of his donkey!

In the Haftarah reading, Micah assails Yisra'el for idolatry and predicts the destruction of Y'rushalayim. The covenant cursings indicate that God will bring exile in order to root out the high places where the toxic impurity of idolatry has poisoned the Land. God shows zeal for His covenant by scattering Yisra'el, to restore true worship to the Land.

In the B'rit Chadashah reading, the call for justice, covenant love, and walking in modesty is pushed further. Yisra'el incurs blindness for steadfastly hardening herself in brotherly hatred. God responds with an act of sheer mercy by opening the eyes of the gentiles to Messiah, even as Yisra'el conspires to crucify the King of the

God shows mercy to the blind.

Jews! Yet He warns the gentiles not to think themselves wise in their own eyes. God reveals a mystery—blindness to His mercy will not only become the basis for the salvation of gentiles, but for the inclusion of Jews as well.

Oasis

. . . Walk Your Talk

Heschel [p. 220, n34] captures the essence of rabbinic thought on the relationship between justice and mercy: ". . . the rabbis remarked that in creating our world, God first intended to rule it according to the principle of strict justice (*middath ha-din*), but He realized that the world could not thus endure so He associated mercy (*middath ha-rahamin*) with justice and made them to rule jointly."

Equity theory contrasts sharply with this rabbinic principle. Each person must carry his own weight, or he is a slacker. Do you keep score when the other guy pulls less than fifty percent and puts the burden on you? Does laziness anger you? Do you find yourself going through life pouting about what isn't fair? Yes, you're right—life *is* unfair. But what are you supposed to do about it?

Messiah proclaims, "Take my yoke upon you and learn from me, because I am gentle and humble in heart, and you will find rest for your souls. For my yoke is easy, and my

> *Be strong in mercy, and your burdens become light!*

burden is light" (Mt. 11:29-30). Determine to live in a more merciful world, and let God judge what's fair and what's not!

 Shabbat Shalom!

So פּינְחָס
upped and took a spear.
He saved Yisra'el
from the plague so near.
It killed many thousands
and caused great fear
that all would die
for a stare and a leer.

Then God made Pinchas
and his sons forever
a holy priesthood
that man cannot sever.
Stay true to God,
oh what an endeavor!
To foreign gods and idols,
always say, "Never!"

Walk PINCHAS!
25:10-29:40(30:1 תג״ך)

Phinehas (dark-skinned)

TORAH—Numbers 25:10-29:40(30:1 תג״ך)

HAFTARAH—1 Kings 18:46-19:21

B'RIT CHADASHAH—Revelation 19:11-21

Inheritance for Pinchas,
an Unlikely Priest

← Looking Back

B'MIDBAR (*in the wilderness of*) Sinai, Moshe counts the army and arranges the camp to flank the tabernacle, using Levites to fence off unholy encroach-ment. Moshe is told, NASO (*elevate!*) special clans to pack and transport the tabernacle. B'HA'ALOT'CHA (*in your making go up*) the lamps, Yisra'el must shine as a light to the nations. The cloud lifts, trumpets signal, the journey begins!

If you can't trust God, SH'LACH L'CHA (*send for yourself!*) spies. But fear of giants sets Yisra'el back a lifetime! KORACH (*Korah/bald*) organizes baldfaced rebellion, gathering jealous firstborns and displaced priests. But God defends Moshe and Aharon as His chosen leaders. The ground swallows Korach's counterfeit mishkan, and 250 leaders are incinerated as they offer incense.

Corpses raise the issue of contamination; thus the need for cleansing by CHUKAT (*the statute of*) the

> **B'MIDBAR** *Sinai, take a census,*
> *arrange the camp, and*
> **NASO** *Levites for holy work—*
> **B'HA'ALOT'CHA** *the lamps,*
> *shine through the night for God!*
>
> **SH'LACH L'CHA** *spies if you must,*
> *but trust God to slay the giants!*
> *Don't sink in* **KORACH***'s jealousy.*
> *God has a place for all, and*
> *that's the bald truth!*
>
> **CHUKAT,** *statutes of, instruction*
> *will keep us pure if we obey.*
> *God's ways are mysterious!*
> *Lifting the bronze serpent saves!*
>
> *Even a donkey knows* **BALAK** *can't*
> *destroy what God will bless!*
> *But idolatry seduces, until*
> **PINCHAS'** *zeal*
> *spears the darkness dead!*

Log

red cow. Grumbling on wilderness detours, the people suffer from the bite of fiery serpents. Mysteriously, gazing on a lifted bronze serpent rescues!

Yisra'el's military success over the Amorites worries **Balak** (*Balak/destroyer*). He hires Bil'am to curse Yisra'el; but the donkey balks, and only blessings pour forth! When that scheme fails, Bil'am suggests seducing Yisra'el into idolatry. Again, plague besets Yisra'el. Then Zimri, a Simeonite prince, brazenly enters the camp with a Midianite princess.

The watchful eye of **Pinchas** (*Phinehas/dark-skinned*) darkens. With zeal for God's zeal, he grabs his spear! He follows the cavorting couple into the inner chamber of the tent, and . . .

In Pinchas . . .

The Key People are Moshe (*Moses*), Pinchas (*Phinehas*), Zimri, Cozbi, Midianites, El'azar (*Eleazar*), the Israelites who were counted second time and listed clan by clan, Kalev (*Caleb*), and Y'hoshua (*Joshua*).

The Scenes are b'arvot Mo'av al-Yarden Y'recho (*on the plains of Moab by the Jordan across from Jericho*); entrance to Tent of Meeting; and har haAvarim (*a mountain in the Abarim range*).

Main Events include Pinchas becoming High Priest because of his zeal; another census count for the army; land inheritance to be based on numbers; Levites receiving no land; note that older generation all gone except Kalev and Y'hoshua; daughters of Ts'lof'chad receiving own inheritance; Y'hoshua dedicated as new leader to succeed Moshe; and regular and festival offerings spelled out.

The Trail Ahead ➡

The Path

וידבר יהוה אל משה לאמר

פּינֹחס בן אלעָזר בן אהרֹן הכֹהֵן

הֵשִׁיב את חמתי מֵעַל בֹּני ישראל

בקנֹאו את קנֹאתי בתוכם

ולא כליתי את בֹּני ישראל בקנֹאתי

—במדבר כה/י-י"א

ס	**חָ**	**נְ**	**י**	**פּ**
letter:	samech	chet	nun	yod	pay
sound:	S	**CHah**	N	EE	Pee

Phinehas (dark-skinned) = Pinchas = **פּינֹחס**

Work

The Legend

And spoke the LORD	va-y'daber ADONAI	וַיְדַבֵּר יְהֹוָה
to Moses, saying,	el-Moshe lemor	אֶל־מֹשֶׁה לֵּאמֹר׃
"Phinehas, son of Eleazar,	Pinchas ben-El'azar	פִּינְחָס בֶּן־אֶלְעָזָר
son of Aaron the priest,	ben-Aharon ha-kohen	בֶּן־אַהֲרֹן הַכֹּהֵן
has turned away	heshiv	הֵשִׁיב
→ wrath-My	et-chamati	אֶת־חֲמָתִי
from on (the) sons of Israel,	me-al b'nei-Yisra'el	מֵעַל בְּנֵי־יִשְׂרָאֵל
in zeal-his	b'kan'o	בְּקַנְאוֹ
→ (for) zeal-My	et-kin'ati	אֶת־קִנְאָתִי
in midst-their,	b'tocham	בְּתוֹכָם
and/so not did I end	v'lo-chiliti	וְלֹא־כִלִּיתִי
→ (the) sons of Israel	et-b'nei-Yisra'el	אֶת־בְּנֵי־יִשְׂרָאֵל
in zeal-My."	b'kin'ati	בְּקִנְאָתִי׃

—Numbers 25:10-11

Related Words

Phinehas, son of El'azar (possible meanings for name include "Negro, dark-complexioned" from Egyptian, "mouth of a snake" from Hebrew, or "southerner," maybe referring to the Nubians in southern Egypt)	Pinchas	פִּינְחָס

Hit the Trail!

The Zealous Inherit God

"... Pinchas the son of El'azar, the son of Aharon the cohen, has deflected my anger from the people of Isra'el by being as zealous as I am, so that I didn't destroy them in my own zeal." —Num. 25:10-11

Pinchas, b'kan'o et kinati (*in his zeal for My zeal*), averts the wrath, "so that I didn't destroy them in My own zeal," says the LORD (Num. 25:11). Kana'a, an Arabic or Syriac word *"to become intensely red,"* indicates the visible effects this angry zeal imprints on a face [Milgrom, p. 216, n11].

God demands exclusive worship (Ex. 20:5). Yet Yisra'el is lured into whoring after Midianite gods. Following the advice of Bil'am, the beautiful Midianite princess, Cozbi (*deceiver*; cf. Fox, Num. 25:15) brazenly seduces Zimri with all Yisra'el watching: "Through the figure of a beautiful woman, many people become corrupted [Yev. 63b]. The evil plan kindles God's wrath; and a fiery plague erupts, killing people by the tens of thousands!

Pinchas inherits an everlasting priesthood.

Bil'am meets a violent end (Num. 31:8). But to Pinchas, who expresses God's wrath, God bestows the b'rit k'hunat olam (*the covenant of eternal priesthood*, Num. 25:13).

Read Dt. 32:21, quotedby Paul in Ro. 10:19. Explain how Yisra'el's turning to idolatry causes God, as it were, to become intensely red with jealousy for His covenant. Explain God's motivation for making gentiles into priests.

Clan Heads Inherit Houses

❝ *[The census results begin with] Re'uven, the first-born of Isra'el. The descendants of Re'uven were: of Hanokh, the family of Hanokhi; of Pallu, the family of the Pallu'i . . .* ❞   —Numbers 26:5

Year forty, the LORD orders Moshe and El'azar to take a census of the clans coming out of the wilderness. Great and distinguished persons are appointed as heads and then listed as separate families, such as the Machirites and the Gileadites.

God orders a census of the next generation.

Tallying all who could serve in the army and are 20 years and upward, the tribes report head counts by clan as follows in the next column:

Tribe	Census 1	Census 2
R'uven	46,500	43,730
Shim'on	52,300	22,200
Gad	45,650	40,500
Y'hudah	54,600	76,500
Yissakhar	54,400	64,300
Z'vulun	57,400	60,500
M'nasheh	32,200	52,700
Efrayim	40,500	32,500
Binyamin	35,400	45,600
Dan	62,300	64,400
Asher	41,500	53,400
Naftali	53,400	45,400
Totals:	603,550	601,730

Thus, the totals diminish by 1820, from 603,550 to 601,730, with the greatest losses from Shim'on and the greatest gains to Y'hudah!

Read Num. 26:12-14, and cf. Num. 1:22-23. Rashi says it appears that all 24,000 who died in the plague (Num. 25:9) were Simeonites. Relate this idea to Zimri's influence. How would you explain the dramatic loss to Shim'on?

Tribal Heads Inherit Land

❝ *ADONAI said to Moshe, "The land is to be parceled out among these as a possession to be inherited, according to the number of names."* ❞

—*Numbers 26:52-53*

Apportion land allotments according to clan arrangement, says God to Moshe. Notably, the census counts 70 clans. God once apportioned all the earth to 70 "sons" descending from Noach (Gen. 10). Now God apportions the Land to the 70 clans of Yisra'el.

Torah states the principle governing apportionment: "to those families with more persons you are to give a greater inheritance, and to those with fewer you are to give a smaller inheritance . . . according to the number counted in it" (Num. 26:54).

A lottery system determines the location of each tribe's land [Num. 26:55-56; B.B. 120a]. L'vi'im are counted separately, but not among those who are assigned a land inheritance, because their inheritance remains the LORD (Num. 26:62; cf. 3:39).

Number each family to determine its inheritance.

The fathers of the first generation, cursed to die in the wilderness, have finally died off completely, just as God swore (Num. 26:64-65).

? *Try to count 70 clans for yourself in Num. 26:5-6, 12-13, 15-17, 19-21, 23-24, 26, 28-33, 35-36, 38-40, 42, 44-45, 48-49, 57-58. Are daughters of Ts'lof'chad included in this count of clans? Are L'vi'im clans included? Do they get land?*

Inheritances Within Clans

❝ ADONAI answered Moshe, "The daughters of Tz'lof'chad are right in what they say. You must give them property to be inherited along with that of their father's brothers . . . ❞   —Numbers 27:6-7

Women do not function within the nation as tribal leaders, clan heads, or even heads of households. Thus, a clan leader, Ts'lof'chad, who dies without sons, will pass on no inheritance!

Generally, male heads of houses inherit land.

The five virgin daughters of Ts'lof'chad petition Moshe to redress a grievance on behalf of their deceased father. Moshe takes the matter directly to the LORD (Num. 27:5).

God agrees that the daughters' request is legitimate. He rules that the daughters can inherit land in this case (Num. 27:7). In fact, the general ruling states that land inheritances should go first to the sons, then to daughters, next to the father's brothers, and after that to close male relatives in the family (Num. 27:8-9). Later, to preserve the integrity of clan inheritances, the daughters will be instructed to marry within their clan (Num. 36:6-9). Marrying outside the clan cedes the land inheritance to another clan.

? Study the LORD's ruling for transfer of inheritances from father to grandson (Num. 27:7-9; cf. Gen. 31:43-47). The procedures governing patrilineal succession are designed to keep ancestral land in the father's line. Comment.

Sanctified Times

❝ ADONAI said . . . "Give an order to . . . Isra'el . . .
'. . . take care to offer me at the proper time the
food presented to me as offerings made by fire, pro-
viding a fragrant aroma for me.'" ❞   —Num. 28:1-2

Throughout the calendar, God appoints specific times for offerings. The children of Yisra'el must start and end each day with olat tamid (*a regular ascent offering*)—a yearling lamb, entirely consumed by fire, along with its accompanying minchah (*tribute*) and nesech (*drink*) offerings (Num. 28:3-8). Thus, each day renews the covenant witnessed by Yisra'el at Mount Sinai under the feet of God (Ex. 24:4-5; Num. 28:6).

The children of Yisra'el must sanctify Shabbat with a double offering, two additional lambs with their accompanying minchah and nesech offerings (Num. 28:9-10).

Sanctify the days, the Shabbats, and the months.

Next, the month is sanctified by offering a minyan of sacrifices: two bulls, a ram, and seven lambs along with their respective minchah and nesech offerings (Num. 28:11-14). Also, a hairy goat is offered as a chatta't (*purification*) in addition to the olat tamid (Num. 28:15).

? ● *Read Num. 28:9-10. The chatta't was omitted on Shabbat and the Amidah shortened, for "no intimation of human wrongdoing is permitted on this joyous day, a principle embodied in the synagogue liturgy" [Levine, p. 241]. Explain.*

Required Offerings

❝ "'In the first month, on the fourteenth day of the month, is ADONAI's Pesach.'" ❞

—Numbers 28:16

Public offerings include a minyan of sacrificial animals. For the New Moon, the seven days of the Feast of Unleavened Bread, Shavu'ot, Rosh haShanah, and Yom Kippur, Torah requires olot (*ascent offerings*) of a bull, ram, and seven lambs, along with a hairy goat as a chata't (*purification*) (Num. 28:19, 22, 27, 30; 29:2, 5, 8, 11).

Do not appear before the LORD empty-handed.

This segment describes two pilgrimage festivals. Pesach prepares for the Feast of Unleavened Bread (Num. 28:16), with convocation days punctuating the start and end (15 to 21 Nisan). Counting the omer begins on 16 Nisan and concludes seven weeks later on Shavu'ot, also called the atseret (*day of restraint*) of Passover. That day, Yisra'el offers new grain to the LORD.

Both of these festivals require a pilgrimage to the sanctuary for mikra kodesh (*holy convocation*). Yisra'el also must abstain from m'lechet avodah (*laborious work*). Preparation of food is permitted, but commercial activities are banned (Num. 28:18, 25).

? Study Num. 28:27, cf. Lev. 23:18. Note the number of bulls and rams to be offered on Shavu'ot. Can you explain the difference? Would you attribute the difference to a copyist error, to a change in the tradition, or to something else?

Offerings for the Nations

❝ "'On the fifteenth day of the seventh month you are to have a holy convocation. You are not to do any kind of ordinary work, and you are to observe a feast to ADONAI seven days.'" ❞ —Num. 29:12

The feast of Sukkot culminates the festival cycle, with more offerings required than on all other festivals combined—double the sheep and rams offered at the Feast of Unleavened Bread; plus seventy bulls, one for each of the seventy sons of Noach, who grew to nationhood! [Sukk. 55b; Gen. 10:32].

Celebrate and feast in the presence of the King!

Thirteen bulls are sacrificed, twelve, . . . on down to seven on the seventh and final day of Sukkot (Num. 29:13, 32).

Rashi explains that offering 14 lambs for each of seven days, a total of 98 lambs, expiates the nation for the 98 curses described in the covenant (Dt. 28:15-68). Multiples of seven, signifying fullness and completion, appear throughout, including 14 rams, 70 bulls, 98 lambs, and seven goats.

Like the Feast of Unleavened Bread, Sukkot lasts seven days; and it commences on a full moon, a convocation day. But attached to Sukkot, a lone bull is offered for Yisra'el on Torah's final convocation day, Sh'mini Atseret (*eighth day of restraint*).

? Says Sifrei 151, "Restrain" from departing with the rest of the nations and spend an extra night in Y'rushalayim!
● "Make a small festive meal for Me, so that I might have pleasure from you" [Sukk. 55b]. Describe Yisra'el's reward.

In Summary

❝ Moshe told the people of Isra'el everything, just as ADONAI had ordered Moshe. ❞

—Numbers 29:40(30:1תג״מ)

Exacting obedience closes out the parashah that elevates Pinchas and his sons to head a mamlechet kohanim v'goy kadosh (*a kingdom of priests and a holy nation*).

> ## *Exacting obedience characterizes the people of God.*

K'chol asher-tsivah ADONAI et-Moshe (*according to all that the LORD commanded Moshe*), now Moshe speaks. Adds Rashi, this ends the word of God to Moshe. Thus, God first calls Moshe to come near. Next, Moshe enters the newly built mishkan (*dwelling*) to hear the word of the LORD. God then instructs Moshe concerning gifts that the children of Yisra'el should bring, when they enter His courts and draw near to Him.

Now, Pinchas and the priesthood are established, the next generation prepares to enter the Land, and a cycle of festivals with required offerings is put in place. The cycle culminates in Sh'mini Atseret, a special little festival reserved for Yisra'el as a *concluding solemnity* (Greek translation in LXX) to be celebrated in the Land.

? Read the end of the rishon and the maftir (Num. 26:1-4, 29:40(30:1תג״מ)), which cover the line of succession for the priesthood and the festival cycles for bringing gifts to the tabernacle. Relate to Ex. 40:19, 21, 23, 25, 27, 30, 32, 33.

A Prophet's Inheritance *Meander*

> **"** *Elisha . . . took the yoke of oxen, slaughtered them, cooked their meat . . . and gave it to the people to eat. Then he got up, went after Eliyahu and became his servant.* **"**
>
> —*1 Kings 19:21*

Zeal for the LORD elevates both Pinchas and Eliyahu (*Elijah*) to national ministry. Like Pinchas, Eliyahu is horror-struck over the introduction of Ba'al worship into life in the nation.

Elisha succeeds Eliyahu in the fight against idolatry.

Eliyahu takes on 450 prophets of Ba'al and orders them all put to the sword. Izevel (*Jezebel*) hears, and she threatens Eliyahu, who runs in despair a day's journey into the Negev to die (1 Ki. 19:4). Twice Eliyahu proclaims his zeal for the LORD, that he is the only one left to openly confront Ba'al worship in Yisra'el (1 Ki. 19:10,14).

God instructs Eliyahu to finish the task. He must anoint Haza'el as king of Aram, Yehu as king of Yisra'el, and Elisha as his successor (1 Ki. 19:15-17). Eliyahu heads to the Jordan Valley and throws his cloak on Elisha as he plows his field.

Elisha responds decisively, sacrificing his plow and oxen to break with his former life (1 Ki. 19:21). Elisha will train with Eliyahu and inherit a double portion of his master's zeal for the LORD (2 Ki. 2:10).

? *Study 1 Ki. 19:10, 14. Eliyahu responds to God's question by saying kano kineiti la-ADONAI (I have been zealously zealous for the LORD). Explain the roles of the sword and the word in the battle against idolatry.*

> **" The rest were killed by the sword that goes out of the mouth of the rider of the horse, and all the birds gorged themselves on their flesh. "**
>
> —*Revelation 19:21*

Heaven opens to make way for the rider called Faithful and True (Rev. 19:11). Scripture depicts the rider as the Messiah, with many royal diadems. He is called the Word of God, also KING OF KINGS and LORD OF LORDS (Rev. 19:13, 16).

End all idolatry.

The Second Coming describes a time when Messiah purges evil in order to set up the kingdom of heaven on earth. He smites the nations with the sharp sword of his mouth (Rev. 19:15, 21). He rules with a rod of iron; and in his zeal, he stains his garments with the blood of those who oppose God's will on earth (Rev. 19:15).

Kayin's killing of Hevel is now measured out to those who oppose Messiah's rulership—whether kings, captains, mighty men, horses, riders, slaves, free, rich, or poor (Rev. 19:18). All who oppose Messiah are slain by the sword of his mouth. They become God's supper for the vultures overhead (Rev. 19:17, 21).

? *Chesed ve'emet attest to God's faithfulness to keep His covenant with the patriarchs (Gen. 24:27, 49; 32:11; 47:29) and with the dynasty promised David (Ps. 89:14, 36(15, 37 רזבי)). What covenant promise does Yeshua inherit?*

Talk Your Walk . . .

PARASHAT PINCHAS elevates the most zealous man to the status of Kohen Gadol, with the promise that his seed will inherit the High Priesthood as an everlasting covenant. The nation is instructed in ways to sanctify time from year to year. Intercession for the nations by the priesthood culminates on Sukkot, when seventy bulls are sacrificed for the seventy nations of the world.

In the Haftarah, the sword of Pinchas' zeal is carried by Eliyahu, who also lives a long life and uses the sword to slay 450 prophets of Ba'al. Eliyahu's zeal for God is unparalleled in his generation. He alone opposes idolatry in Yisra'el. His successor, Elisha, carries on the ministry after God takes Eliyahu in a whirlwind to heaven. It is mankind's only ascension to heaven besides Chanoch, in the days before Noach.

Yeshua displays the same priestly and prophetic zeal against idolatry as Pinchas and Eliyahu, and he also inherits God's covenant kindness and truth to the patriarchs and to David haMelech. Thus, he combines the callings of priest, prophet, and king in the final battle to establish the kingdom of God on earth. To purge evil, he slays those who oppose God's rule with the sword of his mouth! Zeal for the covenant and speaking truth lay the foundations for a new world. Once again God speaks, and a new creation begins! (Heb. 1:1-2).

> *The sword forms,*
> *but the Word transforms.*

Oasis

. . . Walk Your Talk

Holy boldness for God can express itself in a variety of ways. Some swing a sword, some speak out, others fast and pray. You must ask yourself, "In what ways am I zealous for God?"

Prophets have a sensitivity to truth. When truth is violated, the prophet feels stirred to speak out. Do you suffer sudden bursts of emotion when righteous indignation pulses through your veins? Pinchas did, and he slew the ones who plagued the nation and seduced the lustful into abandoning God.

Not everyone has prophetic gifts. But this does not mean you can just shrug and say it's not for you. Yeshua rebuked Satan with the Word of God. Study with zeal! Spend time in Scripture. Learn to slow down in God's

> *Let God's Word overflow your life.*

Presence. Learn to take your time with God. It's a paradox that those who spend quality times in the heavenly places with the Most High also have His ear for the godly burdens they carry.

Do not fool yourself into thinking that you're too busy to slow down and spend time with God. Ask yourself, what is your plan for living out the Word of God?

Shabbat Shalom!

מַטּוֹת are tribes
that make swords from plows.
When facing foreign gods,
one never bows!
Now conquer the enemy,
take all their cows.
Tithe a tenth to the priests,
keep your oaths and vows!

R'uven and Gad,
M'nasheh, go yonder!
Join the other tribes
'cross the Jordan, don't ponder!
Take the Land for God,
it's holy plunder!
Do just as commanded,
let righteousness thunder!

Walk MATOT!
30:1(2-תנ״ך)-32:42

מַטּוֹת

Tribes

TORAH—Numbers 30:1(2-תנ״ך)-32:42

HAFTARAH—Jeremiah 1:1-2:3

B'RIT CHADASHAH—Acts 9:1-22

Tribes Poised for Inheritance

Hiker's

◀ Looking Back

B'MIDBAR (*in the wilderness of*) Sinai, Moshe numbers and arranges the camp to flank the tabernacle from every side, Y'hudah's banner leading the east. With priests in the center, at the tabernacle, Levites fence off any unholiness.

Moshe is told, **NASO** (*elevate!*) special clans to pack and transport the tabernacle en route. God speaks: **B'HA'ALOT'CHA** (*in your making go up*) the lamps, shine as a light to the nations. Blow the trumpets! Move out!! **SH'LACH L'CHA** (*send for yourself!*) spies, but trust God to handle the giants!

Organizing disenfranchised firstborns and priests, baldfaced **KORACH** (*Korah/ bald*) rebels against Moshe and Aharon. But God defends them, and the ground swallows Korach's counterfeit

Number everyone **B'MIDBAR** *Sinai, and arrange the camp.* **NASO** *Levites to guard holiness.* **B'HA'ALOT'CHA** *the lamps, make your light go up as you move out for God.*

SH'LACH L'CHA *spies if you must. But don't fear giants—trust God! When* **KORACH** *sinks in jealousy, support God's chosen leaders!*

Red cows? Bronze serpents? Mysteriously, **CHUKAT** *haTorah can purify and save us.*

BALAK *would destroy what Bil'am would curse, but a donkey balks and God blesses—Mah tovu! The seductive plot darkens 'til* **PINCHAS'** *zeal spears idolatry!*

As the older generation dies, the tribes, **MATOT,** *can prepare to inherit the Land!*

mishkan, along with the households of Dathan and Aviram. More rebels get incinerated as they attempt to offer

Log

incense. Aharon's budding staff reveals God's choice to receive tithes! Two hundred fifty corpses from Korach's rebellion contaminate the camp. Following **CHUKAT** (*the statute of*) the red cow reveals how to cleanse this toxic waste. Statutes work in mysterious ways! Gazing on the lifted serpent saves lives!

BALAK (*Balak/destroyer*) tries to curse Yisra'el. When that fails, Bil'am suggests seducing Yisra'el to covenant with Ba'al. The dark plot fails when **PINCHAS** (*Phinehas/dark-skinned*) shows tremendous zeal for God and spears the idolaters! He becomes Kohen Gadol, an everlasting heritage for his line. Now, the new generation of **MATOT** (*tribes*) stand ready to apportion the Land and enter in conquest . . .

In MATOT . . .

The Key People are Moshe (*Moses*), tribal heads, Midianites, Israelites, Pinchas (*Phinehas*), 5 kings of Midian, Bil'am (*Balaam*), El'azar (*Eleazar*), army officers, Levites, Reubenites, Gadites, Y'hoshua (*Joshua*), family leaders, half-tribe of M'nasheh (*Manasseh*), Amorites, Bashan, Machirites, Ya'ir (*Jair*), and Novach (*Nobah*).

The Scenes include Midianite towns, Mo'av (*Moab*), Tent of Meeting, Ya'azer (*Jazer*), Gil'ad (*Gilead*), list of captured towns, kingdoms of Sichon (*Sihon*) and Og, towns rebuilt in the east, Chavot Ya'ir (*Havvoth Jair*), and K'nat/Novach (*Kenath/Nobah*).

Main Events include laws about husband/wife, father/daughter vows; slaying Midianites and Bil'am, dividing plunder; no casualties, gift of gold; request for grazing territory east of Yarden; warning not to discourage conquest; pledge to help fight in west; and land granted to R'uven, Gad, and M'nasheh.

The Trail Ahead ➡

The Path

וידבר מֹשֶׁה אֶל רָאשֵׁי הַמַּטוֹת

לִבְנֵי יִשְׂרָאֵל לֵאמֹר

זֶה הַדָּבָר אֲשֶׁר צִוָּה יְהוָה

—במדבר ל/ב

ת	ו	ט	מַ
letter: tav	vav	tet	mem
sound: T	**Oh**	Tt	Mah

tribes = MATOT = מַטּוֹת

Work

The Legend

And spoke Moses	*va-y'daber Moshe*	וַיְדַבֵּר מֹשֶׁה
to (the) heads of	*el-rashei*	אֶל־רָאשֵׁי
the <u>tribes</u>	*ha-<u>matot</u>*	הַמַּטּוֹת
of (the) sons of Israel,	*li-v'nei Yisra'el*	לִבְנֵי יִשְׂרָאֵל
saying,	*lemor*	לֵאמֹר
"This (is) the thing	*zeh ha-davar*	זֶה הַדָּבָר
that commanded	*asher tsivah*	אֲשֶׁר צִוָּה
the LORD . . ."	ADONAI	יְהֹוָה:

—*Numbers 30:1(2* תנ״ך)

Related Words

staff, stick, rod, baton, stem, twig, tribe, headquarters	*mateh*	מַטֶּה
personal staff	*mateh ishi*	מַטֶּה אִישִׁי
General Staff	*ha-mateh ha-c'lalee*	הַמַּטֶּה הַכְּלָלִי
headquarters	*mateh rashi*	מַטֶּה רָאשִׁי
bread, staff of life	*mateh lechem*	מַטֶּה לֶחֶם
Note also: bed	*mitah*	מִטָּה

Hit the Trail!

Vows, Oaths, Obligations

❝ Then Moshe spoke to the heads of the tribes of the people of Isra'el. He said, "Here is what ADONAI has ordered: when a man makes a vow . . . he is not to break his word . . . " ❞ —*Numbers 30:1-2(2-3חב״ר)*

Oaths, vows, and obligations invoke the LORD's name. The entire rishon forms a chiasm that grants permission to release women under authority from vows [Milgrom, p. xxii, Num. 30:3-16(4-17חב״ר)].

Tribal heads, fathers, and husbands can annul vows.

The chiasm covers three cases: a female under the authority of her father (vv. 3-5(4-6חב״ר)); a female who makes a vow and later marries (vv. 6-15(7-16חב״ר)); and the laws between a man and his wife (v. 16(17חב״ר)).

Young girls can be released from vows by their fathers, who can annul the vow when they first hear of it [Yad, Ned. 11:7]. Likewise, a husband can release his wife from a vow, when he first hears of it. But silence implies acceptance!

Vows are conditional promises, whereas covenants are promissory oaths. In either event, the result is the same: lo yachel d'varo (*one cannot profane his word*) (Num. 30:2(3חב״ר)). One's word is one's bond.

> *Read Ro. 3:31, cf. Num. 30:3, 4, 7, 11(4, 5, 8, 12חב״ר). Yisra'el is compared to the bride who enters a covenant and becomes part of God's household. Discuss whether God's silence establishes that Torah can be kept by faith.*

Payback!

❝ ADONAI *said to Moshe, "On behalf of the people of Isra'el, take vengeance on the Midyanim. After that, you will be gathered to your people."* ❞

—*Numbers 31:1-2*

Vengeance! God says to punish Bil'am and the Midyanim for seducing Yisra'el away from His covenant. Absolutes exist, and evil must be faced squarely. One can try to seek peace; but once war begins, there's no turning back!

Avenge the covenant!

Avraham once faced five local kings, including the king of S'dom (Gen. 14:7-8). Now Yisra'el faces five local kings, including Tzur, father of Cozbi and tribal leader of Midyan (Num. 31:8 , cf. 25:15). God directs Moshe to draft one thousand men from each of the twelve tribes of Yisra'el, to avenge the seductive intrigues of Bil'am (Num. 31:3-5; cf. Rev. 7:5-8, 14:1-5, 8).

Forces are mustered, and Bil'am is killed, along with all males, including the five local heads of Midyan (Num. 31:8). The women, children, and booty from the households are brought to Moshe, who is furious that those who tried to seduce Yisra'el have not been executed!

Sanh. 106b avers that Pinchas slew Bil'am. The underlying idea is that Bil'am, seeing he could not curse Yisra'el, advised Balak and the Midyanim to seduce Yisra'el. Read Num. 31:2. Why does God say, "Take vengeance!"?

Leaders Rebuked!

> **❝ Moshe, El'azar the cohen, and all the community leaders went to meet them outside the camp. But Moshe was angry with the army officers . . . ❞**
> **—Numbers 31:13-14a**

Moshe cannot understand how the leaders could spare the women who seduced Yisra'el to stray. To be exact, God's zeal for His covenant has already killed 24,000 from Yisra'el! (Num. 31:15, 25:9).

Purify by fire, then decontaminate with water.

Moshe orders the death of every taf (*young male child*) and every woman capable of bearing children (Num. 31:17). Only the taf ba-nashim (*young among the women*) could live (Num. 31:18). Were they C'na'anim, even this act of mercy would be questionable. Surviving Midianite girls are absorbed at the household level; for a nation as a whole cannot be absorbed without absorbing its idolatry, too.

Accordingly, rules are spelled out for decontamination, using the mei niddah (*waters of separation*). All captives are likewise decontaminated. For captives' belongings, immersion purifies; for the captives themselves, such immersion symbolizes conversion (Num. 31:22-23).

? • *Study Num. 31:17-18. Explain how absorbing unblemished female youth into the Yisra'el's households shows kindness to the Midyanim, but still protects Yisra'el from absorbing the idolatry that nearly destroyed the nation.*

Tithe to the Kohanim

❝ *ADONAI said to Moshe, "Take all the booty, both people and animals, you, El'azar the cohen and the leaders of clans in the community; and divide the booty into two parts . . . "* **❞**   —Numbers 31:25-26

Divide the booty from the Midianite victory into equal portions, Yisra'el is commanded. Half goes to the warriors, the other half to the community.

Tithe war spoils seized from the Midyanim.

From the soldiers' portion, a tithe is levied to pay El'azar the kohen one five hundredth of the sheep, cattle, donkeys, and young girls (Num. 31:28-29). Thus, the t'rumat ADONAI (*contribution belonging to the LORD*) for the benefit of the kohanim consists of 675 sheep, 72 cattle, 61 donkeys, and 32 assistants (Num. 31:36-41).

The segment ends with a Hebrew phrase signaling exacting implementation of the orders. This phrase echoes God's instructions to Noach (Gen. 6:22; 7:5); to Avraham (Gen. 21:4); to Moshe and Aharon who direct the nation (Ex. 12:50); and to Moshe, who directs B'tsal'el and Oholi'av (Ex. 36:1), erects the Tabernacle (Ex. 40:19, 21, 23, 25, 27, 29, 32), and elevates the priests (Lev. 8:4). All is done ka'asher tsivah ADONAI et-Moshe (*as the LORD commanded Moses*, Num. 31:41).

? *Recall that the L'vi'im pay tithe on their tithe to the priests (Num. 18:25-29). Notice that citizens tithe, but warriors and L'vi'im only tithe on tithes (Num. 31:28, 36-41, 47; cf. Ex. 30:12). Why the different standards?*

Tithe to the L'vi'im

“ From the half that went to the people of Isra'el, which Moshe separated from that of the men who had gone to fight . . . Moshe took one-fiftieth . . . ”

—Numbers 31:42, 47b

The LORD now directs Moshe to levy a tithe on the community for the L'vi'im (Num. 31:30). Once more, Moshe and El'azar follow the order ka'asher tsivah ADONAI et-Moshe (Num. 31:31).

Exacting obedience generates miraculous results.

Thus, the community tithes to the Levites 6750 sheep, 720 cattle, 610 donkeys, and 320 servants to assist in the duties of the tabernacle. The numbers are ten times the levy assessed on the other half of the malkoach (*spoils*) distributed to the warriors and tithed to the priests. Rashi distinguishes between the spoils and the booty. Baz (*booty*) includes moveable property such as the plunder of personal property, which was not subject to the levy.

The exacting obedience of a faithful, new generation generates its own miraculous fruits. Not a warrior is lost in battle! The army officers personally tell Moshe that the officers had taken a census of those who went to war, and not a man is missing (Num. 31:48-49).

? At Ai, soldiers will die, because Yisra'el is unfaithful in regard to taking property that is banned (Josh. 7:1).
● Again in Acts, people will die, a result of unfaithfulness in giving (Ac. 5:1-11). Relate victorious living to faithfulness.

Sidetracked by Wealth

> **" The descendants of Re'uven and the descendants of Gad had vast quantities of livestock. When they saw that the land of Ya'zer and the land of Gil'ad were good for livestock . . . "**   —Numbers 32:1

What once side-tracked Lot from choosing the Land now sidetracks R'uven and Gad (Num. 32:1, 5, 7-9; cf. Gen. 13:5-13). As firstborns, R'uven and Gad own great herds, and the desire to graze livestock sidetracks them.

Settlement—a new phase in the journey to the Land.

They approach Moshe with a proposal (Num. 32:2-5), which Moshe rejects (Num. 32:6-15; cf. Num. 14:22-23; 32:11). Finally, a compromise is reached (Num. 32:16-19).

Gad will send nechalets (*an advance guard*), 40,000 unencumbered warriors as vanguard commandoes to fight across the Yarden (Josh. 4:13). With numbers from the two and a half tribes at 110,580 (Num. 26:7, 18, 34), two-thirds of the warriors will remain behind to build pens for the livestock and houses for women and children [Levine, p. 270; Rashi on Josh. 22:8]. Men from the nechalets agree not to return until all Yisra'el inherits their place in the Land. R'uven and Gad will then formally receive their inheritance, east of the Yarden (Num. 32:18-19).

? *Read Gen. 13:1-5. Despite having huge quantities of gold, silver, and livestock, explain how Avraham avoided the mistakes his sons committed at Beit-El, Ai, and to the east of the Yarden. How does covenant faithfulness snip sin?*

Conditional Acceptance

❝ Moshe said to them, "If you will do this—if you will arm yourselves to go before ADONAI to the war, . . . then you will be clear . . . and this land here will be yours to possess . . ." ❞ —*Numbers 32:20, 22*

Moshe accepts the obligation Gad and R'uven impose upon themselves. If they cross over and help dispossess Yisra'el's enemies, then they will be n'ki'im (*clear*) of obligation (Num. 32:22).

Negotiate and agree upon obligations with care.

Moshe imposes a negative condition, invoking God's name. Failure to conquer the Land before returning home will bring God's wrath against R'uven and Gad (Num. 32:23). Gad and R'uven agree to do all ka'asher ADONAI m'tsaveh (*as the LORD commands*, Num. 32:25). Stating the full agreement (Num. 32:25-27) and the formula of compromise (Num. 32:28-30), the tribes repeat their acceptance of the terms (Num. 32:31-32).

A public oath before Y'hoshua, El'azar, and the clan heads then grants the Transjordanian lands to Gad, R'uven, and the half-tribe of M'nasheh as an achuzah (*permanent holding*) conditional upon their oath to fight (Num. 32:33-38). So begin the Menassite incursions into the lands of upper Transjordan (Num. 32:39-42).

? *Study the nuances of Num. 32:16, 24, 25-27. Note how Gad and R'uven request to build 'pens and towns.' But*
● *Moshe inverts the order, responding 'towns and pens,' and they agree. Why is this changed order of priority crucial?*

Heirs Cross Over

❝ Novach went and captured K'nat with its villages and named it Novach after himself. ❞

—Numbers 32:42

M'nasheh will conquer inheritances on both sides of the Yarden. M'nasheh's son Machir, his son Gil'ad, and Gil'ad's six sons elect to conquer and settle in Gileadite Transjordan (Num. 26:28-34).

M'nasheh conquers the land of Gil'ad.

Ya'ir and Novach now distinguish themselves as clan leaders when they capture the cities of Gil'ad (Num. 32:41-42). They displace the Amorites, who had displaced the Moabites before them (Num. 32:39, 21:25-26). Ya'ir conquers 23 villages in Gil'ad (1 Chr. 2:22), south of the Yarmok in the Argov region (Dt. 3:14).

Little is known about Novach. Born in Egypt [Sed. OlamR. 9], he conquers K'nat, a town 42 miles east of the Sea of Galilee, and names it after himself (Num. 32:42; cf. Jd. 8:11).

Most importantly, M'nasheh upholds brotherly concerns. Crossing over to fight for Land on both sides of the Yarden, M'nasheh assures his brothers' inheritance.

? Read Num. 32:7-9, 1 Chr. 5:26; cf. Gen. 13:10-11, 14:12. Explain how the one who values cattle more than people will fall short of enjoying long life in the Land. Comment on whether R'uven and Gad repeat Lot's error.

Heirs Are Firstfruits   *Meander*

> **"** *"Isra'el is set aside for Adonai, the firstfruits of his harvest; all who devour him will incur guilt; evil will befall them," says Adonai.* **"**
>
> *—Jeremiah 2:3*

The Haftarot for the next twelve weeks relate to calendar days [Raban]. Tradition attributes the apostasy of the golden calf to the 17 Tammuz, the same day that the outer walls of the Temple were breached by the Romans.

Beware idolatry!

Then follow 21 days to 9 Av, the day both Temples were destroyed. During these three weeks, the *Haftarot of Affliction* warn of the impending doom.

In today's Haftarah, read the week of the 17 Tammuz, Yirm'yahu warns of catastrophe: "Today I have placed you over nations and kingdoms to uproot and to tear down, to destroy and to demolish, to build and to plant" (Jer. 1:10).

Though God remembers Yisra'el's devotion as a bride, first following Him baMidbar "in a land not sown" (Jer. 2:2), now Yisra'el has bowed to other gods and to idols (Jer. 1:16). Even so, she remains holy. Those who devour her will incur God's wrath for eating His firstfruits (Jer. 2:3).

?
● *Study Jer. 1:11-12. The shaked (almond) takes 21 days to go from buds to blossoms. Even so, God shoked (watches over) His word to perform it. Explain how God warns Yisra'el to repent idolatry or face the loss of divine Presence.*

...ings   Our Glorious Inheritance

> " But Sha'ul was being filled with more and more power and was creating an uproar among the Jews living in Dammesek with his proofs that Yeshua is the Messiah. "
>
> —Acts 9:22

Sha'ul obtains letters from the Kohen Gadol to arrest and persecute the Messianic Jews of his time (Ac. 9:1). Zealous for God but blind to Messiah, Sha'ul bears the fruits of the "partial hardening" upon Yisra'el (Is. 6:10).

Sha'ul, a firstfruit of the fathers.

As Sha'ul journeys en route to Dammesek, Yeshua speaks, "I am Yeshua, and you are persecuting me" (Ac. 9:3-5). Sha'ul stands up, but he cannot see. He follows Yeshua's direction to go to a believer's house on Straight Street in downtown Dammesek. There Chananyah prays for him, as instructed in a vision from Yeshua (Ac. 9:10-17). As Chananyah prays for Sha'ul's filling by the Ruach, actual scales pop from Sha'ul's eyes (Ac. 9:18). Sha'ul enters the waters of purification and immediately begins preaching in the synagogues that Yeshua is the Son of God (Ac. 9:20). As the fathers of the rishonim (*first generation*) followed the LORD ba-midbar, now Sha'ul follows Yeshua.

? Read Romans 11:25-27. Do you suppose Paul knew this "mystery" of Yisra'el's partial blindness because he had • experienced it firsthand? Read Dt. 32:21, 28-29 and explain how idolatry can blind one to the mysteries of God.

Talk Your Walk . . .

Parashat MATOT (*tribes*) discusses the power of tribal heads, fathers, and husbands to annul the vows of women in their households. God directs Moshe to kill all Midianites who conspired to seduce Yisra'el into covenant feasts with foreign gods. God's covenant is avenged, and the Midianite women without sin are absorbed. Then God directs the tribes to unite, cross the Yarden, break down the walls, and take the Land.

The Haftarah recalls the wilderness experience as a honeymoon of the LORD with his youthful and devoted bride, Yisra'el. But these times are defiled, because Yisra'el bows to foreign gods and provokes God's wrath. The first of three Haftarot of Affliction is read on 17 Tammuz, the anniversary of the apostasy of the golden calf. Yirm'yahu calls upon Yisra'el to repent or face being absorbed. For failure to repent, the city's walls will be breached, this very same day!

In the B'rit Chadashah, Sha'ul persecutes Jews who believe in Yeshua. He is provoked to anger and even arrests, persecutes, and murders believers. One day, Yeshua calls out to him, and later a believer prays for him in a house in downtown Dammesek. Scales fall from Sha'ul's eyes! Sha'ul now trumpets Yeshua's name in the synagogues. God's kindness to the fathers becomes God's grace to a zealous Sha'ul.

Open your eyes to see!

Oasis

. . . Walk Your Talk

No one is as blind as the one who will not see. Scripture indicates that we are easily sidetracked from focusing on our true inheritance. Are you sober enough most of the time to maintain the awareness that a jealous God watches every move you make?

Rav Sha'ul was enraged by believers. He responded with a campaign to eradicate believers from the face of Yisra'el. He even followed lawful means, garnering letters from the religious authorities and chiefs over the local provinces. Sha'ul had no idea that God had put His own jealousy upon him. Yet fifteen hundred years before, God wrote through Moshe, "I will arouse their jealousy with a non-people and provoke them with a vile nation. 'For my anger has been fired up, it burns to the depths of Sh'ol'" (Dt. 32:21b-22a).

God told us that He would share His divine rage over idolatry so we would know how He felt. Rav Sha'ul knew, all

Belong to God and to God alone.

right. And when his eyes were opened, he proclaimed the Good News in all the synagogues. Sha'ul never cared about his personal well-being after that experience. He cared more for His God. Stop and meditate on how you can show your zeal for God.

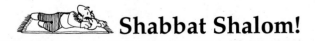 **Shabbat Shalom!**

מַסְעֵי ends the journeys of
wandering Jews,
who trek 40 years
in the same robes and shoes.
Forty-two stops,
in chaos, then order,
from Sinai . . . to Kadesh
. . . to Moab's border.

Zelophehad's heirs,
a five-daughter band,
request of Moshe
to inherit Dad's land.
Moshe asks God
and the ruling comes down,
"Marry in the tribe
to keep your land and town!"

Walk MAS'EI!
33:1-36:13

מַסְעֵי

Journeys of

TORAH—Numbers 33:1-36:13
- 1st Journey through Exile—Numbers 33:1
- 2nd Forty-Two Stops—Numbers 33:11-12a
- 3rd Cross at Jericho—Numbers 33:50-52
- 4th New Generation, New Heads—Numbers 34:16-17
- 5th Forty-Eight Cities—Numbers 35:1-2
- 6th Cities of Refuge—Numbers 35:9-11a
- 7th Marriage Across Tribes—Numbers 36:1
- Maftir End of the Journey—Numbers 36:13

HAFTARAH—Jeremiah 2:4-28; 3:4(Ash.); 4:1-2(Seph.)
- Inherited Blessing—Jeremiah 4:1-2

B'RIT CHADASHAH—James 4:1-10
- Afflictions, Round Two!—James 4:10

An End to the
Wilderness Journeys of Yisra'el

← Looking Back

B'MIDBAR (*in the wilderness of*) Sinai, Moshe counts the army and arranges the camp. With priests in the center at the tabernacle, Levites serve as living fences to keep out unholiness. Moshe is told, NASO (*elevate!*) special clans to pack and transport the tabernacle en route. B'HA'ALOT'CHA (*in your making go up*) the lamps, Yisra'el must shine as a light to the nations. Trumpets blown, it's time to move!

If you can't trust God, SH'LACH L'CHA (*send for yourself!*) spies. But fear of giants can set you back a lifetime! KORACH (*Korah/bald*) rebels, suffering the jealousy of sibling rivalry. Though many perform priestly jobs, Aharon is the only Kohen Gadol.

Following CHUKAT haTorah (*the statute of instruction*) purifies us! Yet even Moshe disobeys over all the whining for water. Lifting the bronze serpent ends the plague, but not the wandering . . .

BALAK (*Balak/destroyer*) tries to curse Yisra'el, when his protectorate,

---

B'MIDBAR Sinai, count the army.
Count Levites separately, and
NASO everyone for special tasks.
B'HA'ALOT'CHA the lamps,
shine as a light to the nations.

Though spies SH'LACH L'CHA,
trust God to protect you. And don't
rebel like baldfaced KORACH!

CHUKAT haTorah keeps you pure.
Though BALAK tries to destroy,
God will bless your tents!
When PINCHAS spears idolatry,
his zeal will change darkness
back to light!

We all belong to MATOT,
each tribe with an inheritance.
The journeys, MAS'EI Yisra'el,
may twist and turn . . .
but God's path holds promise!

Log

Sichon and the Amorites, is defeated. But blessing prevails! "How lovely are your tents, O Ya'akov!"

Bil'am's plot to seduce Yisra'el fails when **Pinchas** (*Phinehas/dark-skinned*) spears the idolaters. His zeal for God's zeal stops the plague and saves the day! His sons will be Kohen Gadol for generations to come.

With the passing of the older generation, **Matot** (*tribes*) apportion the Land in preparation for conquest. Settlers east of the Yarden agree first to help their brothers fight.

Moshe records all 42 stops in the **Mas'ei** (*journeys of*) Yisra'el en route. Establishing borders and cities of refuge prepares for sons and daughters to inherit the Land. As Sefer B'Midbar closes, we camp by the Yarden, ready for final D'varim (*words*)!

In Mas'ei . . .

The Key People are Israelites; Moshe (*Moses*); Aharon (*Aaron*); tribes of R'uven (*Reuben*), Gad, M'nasheh (*Manasseh*); El'azar (*Eleazar*); Y'hoshua (*Joshua*); one leader from each tribe; Gileadite heads, and five daughters of Ts'lof'chad (*Zelophehad*).

The Scenes review wilderness stops (Num. 33:3-49), while on plains of Mo'av (Num. 26:3, 33:50; Dt. 34:1, 8). Other scenes describe borders in new land, Levites' towns, cities of refuge, & land for Ts'lof'chad's daughters.

Main Events include list of journey stops; more traveling; instructions to drive out Canaanites, destroy high places, and divide land; borders of Promised Land; list of leaders to divide inheritance; cities for Levites; cities of refuge; laws about murder; each tribe to pass down own inheritance; and Ts'lof'chad's daughters marrying inside tribe to keep their inheritance.

The Trail Ahead

Compass

The Path

אֵלֶּה מַסְעֵי בְנֵי יִשְׂרָאֵל
אֲשֶׁר יָצְאוּ מֵאֶרֶץ מִצְרַיִם
לְצִבְאֹתָם בְּיַד מֹשֶׁה וְאַהֲרֹן

—בּמדבּר לג/א

מַ	סְ	עֵ	יְ
mem	samech	ayin	yod
Mah	S	(silent)-'ei	EE

letter: sound: (as labeled above)

journeys of = **MAS'EI** = מַסְעֵי

Work

The Legend

These (are the) journeys of	eleh *mas'ei*	אֵלֶּה מַסְעֵי
(the) sons of Israel	v'nei-Yisra'el	בְּנֵי־יִשְׂרָאֵל
that/who went out	asher yats'oo	אֲשֶׁר יָצְאוּ
from the land of Egypt	me-erets Mitsrayim	מֵאֶרֶץ מִצְרַיִם
by hosts/divisions-their	l'tsiv'otam	לְצִבְאֹתָם
by/under (the) hand (of) Moses	b'yad-Moshe	בְּיַד־מֹשֶׁה
and Aaron.	v'Aharon	וְאַהֲרֹן

—Numbers 33:1

Related Words

journey, travel, march, trek, departure, campaign, rally	masa	מַסָּע
maiden voyage (trip firstling)	masa b'chorah	מַסָּע בְּכוֹרָה
quarried stone (stone transported)	ehvehn masa	אֶבֶן מַסָּע
travel books, travelogues	sifrei masa'ot	סִפְרֵי מַסָּעוֹת
passport (trip document)	t'udat masa	תְּעוּדַת מַסָּע
transported, conveyed	musa	מֻסָּע
bon voyage, have a good trip	n'siah tovah	נְסִיעָה טוֹבָה!
to take (arrange) a journey	arach masa	עָרַךְ מַסָּע

Hit the Trail!

Journey through Exile

❝ These are the stages in the journey of the people of Isra'el as they left the land of Egypt divided into groups under the leadership of Moshe and Aharon.❞

—Numbers 33:1

Moshe records each stage in MAS'EI b'nei Yisra'el (*the journeys of the sons of Yisra'el*), listing the starting points beginning with the exodus from Egypt. Three divisions stand out: 12 stops from Ra'amses to Sinai (Num. 33:5-15); 21 stops from Sinai to Kadesh (Num. 33:16-36); and nine stops from Kadesh to the steppes of Mo'av (Num. 33:37-49).

On 15 Nisan, 2448 (1313 BCE), Yisra'el departed Ra'amses b'yad ramah (*with a high hand*), on their way to Sukkot [Kantor, p. 26; Num. 33:3, 5; Ex. 12:37, 14:8]. As Egypt buried her firstborns, God destroyed Egyptian idols (Ex. 12:12).

March from Egypt into the wilderness.

The journey continued to Etam and then on to Freedom Valley facing Ba'al Ts'fon, the last Egyptian idol [Num. 33:6-8; Ex. 14:2-4; *Walk Exodus!*, p. 71]. Crossing the sea on 21 Nissan, Yisra'el gaped as the deep swallowed Pharaoh's army. Yisra'el journeyed three more days ba-midbar to Marah, then on to Elim and Yam Suf (Num. 33:10).

Read Num. 33:1-49, which reviews Yisra'el's journey from Egypt to Sinai (Num. 1:1-10:10), Sinai to Kadesh (Num. 10:11-20:13), and Kadesh to Mo'av (Num. 20:14-36:13). Would you title this book NUMBERS or B'MIDBAR?

Forty-Two Stops

❝ *They moved on from the Sea of Suf and camped in the Seen Desert. They moved on . . .* ❞

—Numbers 33:11-12a

Moshe's master list details Yisra'el's journey B'MIDBAR (*in the wilderness of*) Sinai. The record accounts for the itinerary of a military campaign, with emphasis on military exploits, tribute, sources of water, and river crossings.

March through the wilderness for 38 years.

The march continued from Yam Suf (*the Sea of Reeds*) to the Sin Desert (Ex. 16:1), a place with tamarisk groves and high humidity. On to Dophka, the itinerary can then be roughed out as follows [Shulman, p. 79]:

Alush	15 Iyar, 2448
R'fidim	23 Iyar, 2448
Sinai Desert	1 Sivan, 2448
depart Sinai	20 Iyar, 2449

En route from Sinai, three stops occur before the scouts return. Then follow another eighteen stops in eighteen years to reach Kadesh (Num. 33:18-36), where Yisra'el stays for 19 years.

Aharon dies at Mount Hor in the fortieth year on 1 Av [Shulman, p. 80; Num. 33:37-38]. Eight stops later, Yisra'el reaches the steppes of Mo'av, the final stop.

? *Notice B'MIDBAR and NASO occur in year 1, B'HA'ALOT'-CHA through KORACH in year 2, CHUKAT in years 2-40, and MAS'EI still in year 40. Challenge! Defend these calculations: Num. 19:22-20:1 = 38 years; Num. 20:1-22 = same year.*

Cross at Jericho

> ❝ ADONAI *spoke to Moshe in the plains of Mo'av by the Yarden, across from Yericho* ... *"When you cross the Yarden into the land of Kena'an, you are to expel all the people* ... " ❞ —Numbers 33:50-52

Begin conquest and apportion the Land! This segment delimits the boundaries of C'na'an as corresponding to those of an Egyptian province in the fifteenth to the thirteenth century BCE [Num. 34:1-15; Fox, p. 826; Milgrom, p. 284].

Dispossess the C'na'anim and inherit the Land!

Yisra'el must implement the divine command to annihilate all Canaanites. God warns Yisra'el that survivors will be sikim (*barbs*) in their eyes, ts'ninim b'tsideichem (*spines in your sides*), v'tsararu et-chem (*and they will assault you*) (Num. 33:55). In fact, says the LORD, "as I thought to do to them, so I will do to you!" (Num. 33:56).

Tribal inheritances will be apportioned by lot [Rashi]. Functioning as guardians for their tribes, leaders will apportion suitable amounts to clans and individuals according to the principle, "for the many, you are to make-much ... for the few, you are to make-little their inheritance" (Fox, Num. 33:54, 26:52-56).

> ❓ *Study 1 Ki. 9:20-21. Neither Israelite efforts (Num. 33:52-56) nor divine agency (Ex. 23:20-31) alone prevails. Give your view of how fate and free will play out in history. Read Josh. 23:13 and relate exile to the curses of the covenant.*

New Generation, New Heads

> ❝ ADONAI *said to Moshe, "These are the names of the men who will take possession of the land for you: El'azar the cohen and Y'hoshua the son of Nun."* ❞
>
> —Numbers 34:16-17

El'azar and Y'hoshua oversee apportionment of the Land, assisted by one nasi (*exalted leader*) from each tribe except Gad and R'uven. They inherit lands mizrachah (*on the east* or *sunward*), across the Yarden (Num. 34:15).

El'azar, who advises Y'hoshua, is listed first. Both men oversee the apportionments, standing in the place formerly occupied by Aharon and Moshe. Among the tribal leaders, Y'hudah comes first (having replaced R'uven as first among equals). The rest of the leaders in Num. 34 have changed from those named in Num. 13. Except for Kalev and Y'hoshua, the other leaders have died out, as sworn by the LORD (cf. Num. 14:37-38).

Apportion the Land to every clan.

When the new generation crosses over, they must still conquer the lands apportioned to them. Each tribal leader acts as agent l'nachel (*to parcel out*) land for families and individuals. Their actions are binding, with no grounds for appeal [Rashi].

> ❓ Yisra'el's uniqueness among the nations can be seen in its calling as a collective of households (Ex. 1:1). Read Num. 34:1-2a, 16-29. Explain how tribal leaders function as heads of households for their respective tribes.

Forty-Eight Cities

❝ In the plains of Mo'av by the Yarden, across from Yericho, ADONAI said to Moshe, "Order the people of Isra'el to give to the L'vi'im . . . some of the open land surrounding the cities. ❞ —Numbers 35:1-2

Set aside forty-eight cities for L'vi'im—including six cities of refuge, three on each side of the Yarden. So the tribes are told to provide cities for the L'vi'im in their midst. In turn, the L'vi'im role model exemplary lives devoted to God [Stone, p. 927].

Give Land to the L'vi'im.

Levitical cities consist of the city proper, the migrash (*open space*) surrounding the city, and fields and vineyards surrounding the migrash.

The migrash reserves pristine land to beautify the environment surrounding the city. No building or agriculture is permitted on the migrash [Rashi]. Rather, the migrash provides space for animals (riding), for cattle and sheep (grazing), and for added needs (beehives, pigeons) [Sforno, p. 820].

Commentators vary in their estimates of areas. The city is 1000 square cubits; but the migrash adds an additional 500-1000 cubits on each side, and fields and vineyards add yet another 1000-2000 cubits per side.

❓ Read Num. 35:8 with care. Rashi says that larger tribes received more land. Ramban says each tribe received equal portions. Scan Joshua 21. Explain whether the larger tribes gave L'vi'im more land or more valuable land.

Cities of Refuge

" ADONAI said to Moshe, "Tell the people of Isra'el, 'When you cross the Yarden into the land of Kena'an, you are to designate for yourselves cities that will be cities of refuge ... '" **—Num. 35:9-11a**

C ities of refuge provide access to those fleeing homicide and being pursued by the go'el ha-dam (*redeemer of the blood*), a blood relative of the murdered.

> *Provide sanctuary only for those who murder unintentionally.*

Unrequited blood defiles the land (Num. 35:33-34). The city of refuge provides sanctuary protection for the murderer, until a court can determine whether the murder was committed in a pre-meditated way (Num. 35:12).

The go'el ha-dam restores the debt of blood. It is not just the blood of the slain that cries out from the ground for justice (Gen. 4:10-11). God also demands accountability (Gen. 9:5-6; Ps. 9:12 (13תהל״ים); Dt. 21:1-9). He Himself will abandon the Land if the spilling of human blood goes unrequited (Mt. 23:35-38).

M'nasheh, R'uven, and Gad all receive cities of refuge (Dt. 4:41-43). Three more lie across the Yarden at Kedesh in Galil, Sh'chem in Efrayim, and Chevron in Y'hudah (Josh. 20:7-8; Num. 35:13-14).

Read Num. 35:33-34, Lev. 25:29-34. The go'el ha-dam's role includes redressing the twin horrors of defiled land and lost land. Study Ro. 11:26-27. Describe the role of the nation's Go'el on the Day of Redemption.

Marriage Across Tribes

" The leaders of the clans of the family of the descendants of Gil'ad, . . . son of M'nasheh . . . of the descendants of Yosef, approached and addressed Moshe and the leaders . . . " —Numbers 36:1

The heads of Gil'ad speak to Moshe and the rest of the leaders of Yisra'el (Num. 36:1). They express concerns that their tribe can lose allotted inheritances, if their women heirs intermarry with other tribes (Num. 27:7).

Protect the inheritance for future generations.

The leaders complain that even the Yovel will not protect them from this outcome. Moshe listens to their concerns and agrees (Num. 36:4).

Consulting with the LORD, Moshe revokes the decree and permits tribal intermarriage [Taan. 30b]. But he instructs the daughters of Ts'lof'chad to cleave to their father's inheritance (Num. 36:6-7). The rule is generalized for subsequent female heirs, so that every Israelite possesses nachalat avotav (*the inheritance of his fathers*) (Num. 36:8-9). The daughters comply, marrying within their clan to assure an orderly future within the Land— ka'asher tsivah ADONAI et-Moshe (*as the LORD commanded Moshe*) (Num. 36:10).

? Often MATOT/MAS'EI is read together as a double portion. How does Num. 36:1-3,6 differ from Num. 27:1-4,8? What ruling is amended? Concerning household authority, explain the roles of clan and tribal leaders, Moshe, and God.

End of the Journey

> **" These are the mitzvot and rulings which ADONAI gave through Moshe to the people of Isra'el in the plains of Mo'av by the Yarden, across from Yericho. "**
> —Numbers 36:13

Yisra'el camps upon the steppes of Mo'av by the Yarden, overlooking Y'recho. The tribes will not move from the this spot for the rest of Sefer B'MIDBAR, nor for all of Sefer D'VARIM! Thus concludes Yisra'el's journey through the wilderness.

A major bracket knits together Num. 26:52 and Num. 36:13. The discourse quotes God's words to Moshe on the steppes of Mo'av. What starts with the daughters approaching Moshe and El'azar (Num. 27:1-2) concludes with a clan discussion.

The journey ends with the heiresses marrying within the clan out of obedience, so that keeping the Land within the clan will assure an orderly future for land inheritances.

Wilderness wanderings finally end.

Sefer B'MIDBAR closes with the sons of Yisra'el camped on the border of the Promised Land. The stage is set for Moshe's final words of prophecy and exhortation, as a new generation readies itself to conquer the Land!

? Read Num. 36:11, cf. Num. 27:1. Explain why No'ah, the wiser and younger sister of Tirzah, is placed first. Why are the names switched in Num. 36:11? How does switching the names define the bracket [Num. 26:52; Num. 36:13]?

Inherited Blessing   *Meander*

> ❝ *Isra'el, if you will return ... and if you will swear,*
> *"As ADONAI lives," in truth, justice and righteous-*
> *ness; then the nations will bless themselves by him,*
> *and in him will they glory.* ❞   —*Jeremiah 4:1-2*

God asks how Yisra'el could forget the honeymoon days of the wilderness. How could the fathers pursue hevel (*naught*)? How could they all fail to ask, Ayeh ADONAI (*where is the* LORD)? (Jer. 2:6, 8)

Man has forsaken the fount of living water and become prey for lions (Jer. 2:13, 15). God's people have become a gefen nochriyah (*alien vine,* Jer. 2:21). Consequences of hardening have changed the very nature of the people of God!

Yisra'el has perished and Y'hudah has changed.

Yet all is not lost. Y'hudah can still repent, recover the honeymoon experience, and say with sincerity, "My Father! You are my friend from my youth!" (Jer. 3:4). Then the nations will bless themselves and the blessings, not the cursings, of the covenant will come to fruition (Jer. 4:1-2).

Man's disloyalty stuns God (Jer. 2:5). How could the fathers stray so far from the covenant relationship and not even ask a question? God appeals to heaven (Jer. 3:12).

> ❓ *Read Jer. 2:6, 8-9; cf. Gen. 3:9, 4:9. Explain how God asks*
> *questions when honeymoons in Gan Eden and later with*
> *the wandering generation fall on hard times, but man*
> *does not learn by God's example. What consequences result?*

...*ings*   **Afflictions, Round Two!**

> **" Wail, mourn, sob! Let your laughter be turned into mourning and your joy into gloom! Humble yourselves before the Lord, and he will lift you up. "**
> —James 4:10

One cannot serve God and carnal man at the same time. Desires of the inner man lead to quarrels and fights among men (Jas. 4:1). Frustration escalates into warfare (Jas. 4:2). Prayers go unanswered, because prayers to indulge the flesh are fruitless (Jas. 4:3).

Quoting from the Septuagint translation of Prov. 3:34, James states, "God opposes the arrogant, but to the humble he gives grace." Indeed, the grace God gives is greater (Jas. 4:6). God has put His Spirit in us to combat human jealousy (Jas. 4:5b). Either the Ruach roots out our carnal desires, or we will bite and devour one another. Double-mindedness is not an option (Jas. 4:8).

Be exalted in repentance or be cast down in affliction.

When convicted of sin, we should repent with fullness of heart, accompanied by distress, sorrows, and even the shedding of tears (Jas. 4:9-10). Without complete repentance, pain and suffering from afflictions is the only choice we leave a holy God.

> **? "If one say, 'I will sin and repent, I will sin and repent,' he will not be given an opportunity to repent. 'I will sin and the Day of Atonement will effect atonement,' then ... [it] does not effect atonement." [M. Yoma 8:9]. Comment.**

Talk Your Walk . . .

Wandering B'MIDBAR (*in the wilderness of*) Sinai ends! Forty-two stops detail MAS'EI (*the journeys of*) Yisra'el, as the old guard dies off and the new generation prepares for entry.

The 43rd haftarah is read as the second of three Haftarot of Affliction, warning of the destruction of the Temple and of Y'rushalayim. Yisra'el has been devoured and exiled, but Y'hudah has not learned. In fact, Y'hudah has not even asked, "Where is the LORD?" God says that Y'hudah is no longer the tender vine who spoke to Him as "Father." Now Y'hudah has become an "alien vine." There can be no whole-hearted repentance by one who has been hardened by the effects of sin. Y'hudah must see what's happened, recover the covenant relationship with God as Father, and repent with wholeness of heart!

The B'rit Chadashah continues the thrust of how hardening changes one's nature. James comments that the inner man cannot set itself upon pursuing the passing pleasures of sin. Such unfulfilled desires escalate into jealousies and murderous impulses which bear poisonous fruits. One cannot have it both ways—either one serves God, or one hardens into friendship with the world and enmity with God. When full-hearted repentance becomes impossible, only suffering can restore the lost virtues that undergird repentance.

Always maintain tenderness of heart towards God.

Oasis

. . . Walk Your Talk

Lessons of the covenant must never be forgotten. Leviticus warns those who are pining away in the lands of the enemies:

"Then they will confess their misdeeds and those of their ancestors which they committed against me. At that time I will be going against them, bringing them into the lands of their enemies. But if their uncircumcised hearts will grow humble, and they are paid the punishment for their misdeeds; then I will remember my covenant with Ya'akov,

> *Enter the Land with a circumcised heart.*

also my covenant with Yitz'chak and my covenant with Avraham; and I will remember the land. For the land will lie abandoned without them, and it will be paid its Shabbats while it lies desolate without them; and they will be paid the punishment for their misdeeds . . . " (Lev. 26:40-43).

Note that confession led to further affliction! Punishment accomplishes two purposes: Yisra'el's "uncircumcised" heart grows humble, and the Land is paid back its Sabbaths without being defiled by a people with an uncircumcised heart.

Is your heart tender to God? Are you sensitive to the horrors of sin? It is not suffering, but a circumcised heart that brings you near to God, your Father. How can you keep your heart circumcised for God?

 **Shabbat Shalom!**

Crossing into the Promised Land carries the hopes of returning to the lost Paradise of Gan Eden. The covenant promises long life in the Land. Yisra'el will be fruitful, multiply, fill the earth, and subdue it. She will rest on Shabbats and inherit the lands of those who attack her (Gen. 22:17-18).

But idolizing other gods poses threats to the new generation. Yisra'el will descend from her high calling among the nations. The cycle of cursing passes the sins of the fathers across generations in a downward spiral—a

Walk in blessing and rule with God!

spiritual DEAD end culminating in destruction, exile, assimilation, and the death of nationhood. Can "life from the dead" (Ro. 11:15) and the resurrection of the house of Yisra'el (Jer. 31:31-33(30-32 הנב)) follow?

The major prophets come to Y'hudah and warn her sternly. They implore her to learn the lessons of Torah, with its legal instruction concerning the consequences of disobedience. If Y'hudah will not learn from Torah, she should take heed from the dead end of her sister nation, Yisra'el.

Alas, Y'hudah stands blinded by her sins and deaf to her prophets! Yet the Eternal One pleads, ". . . if you return to Me and remove your abominations from before Me, and do not go astray, and if you swear by the living God in truth, justice, and righteousness, then nations shall find blessing in you, and glory in you" (Plaut, Jer. 4:1-2; cf. Gen. 22:17-18, 26:4).

End

Sefer B'MIDBAR concludes with a nation perched on the steppes of Mo'av, awaiting instructions to cross over and enter the Promised Land. Today believers stand perched at the gateway of the millennium, separated only by the same problems that confront Yisra'el: the world, the flesh, and the Adversary.

Are you willing to go the next mile with clean hands and a pure heart? Will you face the idols that hang up your progress to the Promised Land? Can you confront the giants in your life? Will you trust God for the victory? Ponder the words of the great prophet, Yesha'yahu: "Thus someone on earth who blesses himself will bless himself by the God of truth . . ." (Is. 65:16a).

Perhaps you face awesome problems, such as keeping a steady discipline of diet and regular exercise to give you the vitality to pray. Maybe you face immense psychological difficulties, such as a paternalistic family that has no tolerance for your beliefs or life circumstances. Perhaps you are prone to depression or loneliness.

> *Return with a full-heart, and walk with God!*

Your particular human weakness must not control your life! Exercise your priestly freedom to draw near to God. Pray with fervency, and ask your Father to make you whole. How will you respond to God's call to take the Promised Land? The choice is yours.

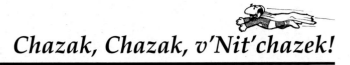

Chazak, Chazak, v'Nit'chazek!

We stop to rest
on Moab's plains,
and gaze at
promised fields of grains.
Yet the beat goes on,
let the Torah roll.
Deuteronomy!
The end of the scroll!
After wandering,
we take a break.
Chazak, Chazak, v'Nit'chazek!

חֲזַק חֲזַק וְנִתְחַזֵּק
*Be strong, be strong,
and may we be strengthened!!!*

Glossary

ACHAREI **MOT** (*after the death*)

ach et ha-da**var** asher-ada**ber** **elei**cha oto ta'**a**seh (*but the word that I speak to you, that you will do!*)

ach**u**zah (*permanent holding*)

ADONAI (*the* LORD)

ADONAI-Tsva'**ot** (*the* LORD *of Hosts/Armies*)

Aha**ron** (*Aaron*)

al**fei** Yisra'el (*the thousands of Israel*)

ali**yah** (*go up*)

al pi ADONAI (*according to the mouth of the* LORD)

ameta**mel**eytos (Greek for *not-with-sorrow/regret*)

Ami**dah** (*standing* prayer)

'A**mon** (*Ammon*)

a**sah** e**met** (*do the truth*)

a**sham** (*reparation*)

Ashke**naz**im (Jews of middle and northern European descent; abbrev. Ash.)

A**shur** (*Assyria*)

at**ser**et (*day of restraint*)

a**vel** (*wrong*)

Avi**hu** (*Abihu*)

Avi**ram** (*Abiram*)

avo**dah** (*service*)

avo**dat** O**hel** Mo'**ed** (*service of the Tent of Meeting*)

a**vot** (*fathers*)

A**yeh** ADONAI (*Where are you,* LORD*?*)

Ba'al (*Baal, lord, husband*)

Ba'al-P'**or** (*Lord of Baring*)

BA**LAK** (*Balak/destroyer*)

ba-mid**bar** (*in the wilderness*)

Ba**mot** **Ba'**al (*Bamoth Baal/High Places of Baal*)

b'ar**vot** Mo'**av** al-Yar**den** Y're-**cho** (*on the plains of Moab by the Jordan across from Jericho*)

baz (*booty*)

BCE (Before the Common Era)

B'CHU**KO**TAI (*in My statutes*)

Beit-El (*Bethel*)

ben ba**kar** (*son of the herd*)
b'**e**ver ha**Y**ar**den** (*across the Jordan*)
B'HA'ALOT'CHA (*in your making go up*)
B'HA'ALOT'CHA et ha-ne**rot** (*in your making go up the lamps*)
B'**HAR** (*on the Mount*)
bik**ku**rim (*first-ripe fruits*)
Bil'**am** (*Balaam*)
Bin**ya**min (*Benjamin*)
b'kan'**o** et kina**ti** (*in his zeal for My zeal*)
B'MIDBAR (*in the wilderness or in the wilderness of*)
B'MIDBAR Sinai (*in the wilderness of Sinai*)
b'**nei** Yisra'**el** (*the children of Israel*)
BO (*enter!*)
B'REISHEET (*in the beginning*)
B'**rit** Chada**shah** (*New Covenant*/New Testament)
b'**rit** k'hu**nat** o**lam** (*the covenant of eternal priesthood*)
B'SHALACH (*when he let go*)
b'**yad** ra**mah** (*with a high hand*)
chaga**vim** (*locusts*)
chai a**ni** (*as I live*)
chal**lah** (*a loaf*)
Chanan**yah** (*Ananias/ God is gracious*; also Chanan**ya**hu/ *Hananiah*)
Chat**se**rot (*Hazerot*)

chat**ta't** (*sin offering, purification*)
Cha**vot** Ya'**ir** (*Havvoth Jair*)
CHAYEI SARAH (*the life of Sarah*)
Chaza'**el** (*Hazael*)
Cha**zak**, cha**zak**, v'nitcha**zek** (*Be strong, be strong, and may we be strengthened*)!!!
Chen! Chen! (*Grace! Grace!*)
che**sed** (*covenant kindness*)
che**sed** ve'**emet** (*covenant kindness and truth*)
Chev**ron** (*Hebron*)
chil**lel** (*profane*)
Chor**mah** (*Hormah/ destruction*)
Cho**vav** (*Hobab/Jethro*)
CHUKAT (*statute of*)
chu**kim** (*statutes*)
C'**na**'an (*Canaan*)
C'na'**anim** (*Canaanites*)
co**hen**/coha**nim**—see ko**hen**
Coz**bi** (*deceiver*)
Dam**me**sek (*Damascus*)
Da**tan** (*Dathan*)
Da**vid** ha**Me**lech (*King David*)
dibar**tem** el ha-**se**la' (*speak to the rock*)
di**bat** ha'**aretz** (*a bad report of the Land*)
dor l'**dor** (*generation to generation*)
Efra**yim** (*Ephraim*)
ek**kle**sia (*Greek for church*)
El'**azar** (*Eleazer*, also *Lazarus*)
El El**yon** (*God the Most High*)

el ha-kubbah (*into the innermost chamber/"womb"*)

Elitsafan (*Elizaphan*)

Eliyahu (*Elijah*)

Elitsur (*Elizur*)

el-kovotahh (*into her womb*)

EMOR (*say!*)

Eshta'ol (*Eshtaol*)

Etam (*Etham*)

Gan Eden (*the Garden of Eden/Paradise*)

gefen nochriyah (*alien vine*)

ger (*resident sojourner, stranger*)

gerim v'toshavim (*sojourners and resident-settlers*)

ger toshav (*resident-settler*)

Gil'ad (*Gilead/Rugged Country*)

go'el (*redeemer, kinsman redeemer*)

go'el ha-dam (*redeemer of the blood*)

goyim (*gentiles, nations*)

Gulgolta (*Golgotha/Place of the Skull*)

HA'AZINU (*give ear!*)

haChitti (*Hittites*)

haC'na'ani (*Canaanites*)

haEmori (*Amorites*)

hafshet (*strip!*)

Haftarah (*conclusion/ Prophets and Writings*)

Haftarot (pl. of Haftarah)

Halachah/Halakhah (*Hebrew Law*)

haL'vi'im (*the Levites*)

ha-m'at? (*is it too little?*)

ha-n'chashim ha-s'rafim (*the fiery serpents*)

har haAvarim (*a mountain in the Abarim range*)

hatsnea lechet (*walk in modesty*)

haY'vusi (*Jebusites*)

he'alu misaviv l'mishkan-Korach, Datan, va-Aviram (*go up from around the dwelling of Korah, Dathan, and Abiram*)

hemah mei m'rivah (*these are the Waters of Quarreling*)

heromu . . . va'achaleh otam k'raga (*move aside . . . and I will devour them in an instant!*)

hevel (*naught, transitory*)

Hevel (*Abel, transitory*)

hibad'lu . . . va'achaleh otam k'raga (*separate yourselves . . . and I will devour them in an instant!*)

hikdashti (*I made holy/sanctified to myself*)

hit'yats'vu oo-r'u et-y'shuat ADONAI (*stand fast and see the salvation/Yeshua of the LORD*)

Hor haHar (*Mt. Hor*)

Hoshea (*Hosea*)

ish nachalat avotav (*each man [possesses] the inheritance of his fathers*) ish tahor (*clean person*)

Itamar (*Ithamar*)

Iyar (second month in the Hebrew calendar)

Izevel (*Jezebel*)

jihad (*holy war*)

ka'asher ADONAI m'tsaveh (*exactly as my LORD commands*)

ka'asher tsivah ADONAI et Moshe (*as the LORD commanded Moshe*)

kach matteh (*take a staff*)

kach . . . v'hoka otam la-ADONAI neged ha-shamesh (*take . . . and impale them before the LORD against the sun*, i.e. *publicly*)

kadesh (*sanctification*)

Kalev (*Caleb*)

kana'a (Arabic or Syriac, "*to become intensely red*," related to kan'o kineiti below)

kano kineiti la-ADONAI (I have been zealously zealous for the LORD)

karet (*being cut off*)

karev (*encroachment*)

kashrut (*kosher laws*)

Kayin (*Cain*)

k'chol asher-tsivah ADonai et-Moshe (*according to all that the LORD commanded Moshe*)

K'DOSHIM (*holy ones*)

k'dushah (*a state of holiness*)

ketsef (*wrath*)

K'hat (*Kohath*)

Kiryat Chutsot (*Kiriath Huzoth*)

KI TISA (*when you elevate*)

Kivrot-haTa'avah (*Kibroth Hattaavah/ graves of craving*)

K'nat/Novach (*Kenath/Nobah*)

kodesh kodashim (*Holy of Holies; especially holy offerings*)

kohanim/cohanim (*priests*)

kohen/cohen (*priest*)

Kohen Gadol (*High Priest*)

Kohen haGadol (the *High Priest*)

kol adat Yisra'el (*the whole community of Israel*)

kol ha-edah (*all the community*)

kolot (*voices*)

KORACH (*Korah/bald*)

kosher (Ashkenazi)/kasher (Sephardic) (*fit, fit for eating*)

k'ruvim (*cherubim*)

"Kuma, ADONAI" (*Rise up, LORD*)

k'valla (*for as long as it takes to swallow*)

kvetching (Yiddish for *complaining*)

Kum (*arise!*) . . . Ha'azinah (*give ear!*)

la'avod et avodat ha-mishkan (*to do the work/service/worship of the dwelling*) la'avod et avodat Ohel Mo'ed (*to serve the service of the the Tent of Meeting*)

l'daber ito (*to speak with Him, i.e. conversing/conferring with*)

LECH L'CHA (*go forth, yourself!*)

l'gul'g'lotam (*by their skulls*)

l'ha'alot he'anan (*when the cloud lifted up*)

lifnei ADONAI (*before the* LORD)

Lo-'Ammi (*Not My People*)

lo na'aleh (*we will not go up!*)

l'nachel (*to parcel out*)

lo alah aleha 'ol (*never go up upon her a yoke*)

Lo-Ruchamah (*No Mercy*)

lo yachel d'varo (*one cannot profane his word*)

L'vi'im (*Levites*)

L'vo Chamat (*Lebo Hamath*)

LXX (Septuagint, Greek trans. of Heb. Scriptures)

ma'aser (*tithe, tenth*)

ma'aser min ha ma'aser (*tenth within the tenth*)

maftir (*concluding*)

mah tov (*what is good*)

mah tovu (*how goodly*)

mamlechet kohanim v'goy kadosh (*kingdom of priests and a holy nation*)

manna (from "man," Egyptian for *gift* or *coming from the sky every day*; see Ex. 16:14-15)

MAS'EI (*journeys of*)

MAS'EI b'nei Yisra'el (*the journeys of the sons of Yisra'el*)

MATOT (*tribes*)

matteh (*staff*)

me'ever l'Yarden (*from across the Jordan*)

Meidad (*Medad*)

mei niddah (*waters of separation*)

midbar (*wilderness*)

Midbar-Tsin (*Desert of Zin*)

middath ha-din (*measure of justice*)

middath ha-rahamin (*measure of mercy*)

midot k'neged midot (*measure for measure*)

Midrash (*inquiry, rabbinical commentary on the Bible*)

midrash (study, sermon, homiletic interpretation)

Midyan (*Midian*)

Midyanim (*Midianites*)

migrash (*open space*)

MIKETZ (*at the end of*)

mikra kodesh (*holy convocation*)

mille yadam (ordination, lit. *filling their hands*)

minchah (*grain offering, tribute, meal offering*)

minchat bikkurim (tribute of first-processed)

minyan (lit. *number/quorum of 10 adults for public prayer*)

Miryam (*Miriam*)

mish**kan** (*tabernacle/God's dwelling*)

mish**kan** edut (*dwelling of testimony*)

mish**me**ret (*military guard duty*)

Mish**nah** (*teachings, the Oral Law compiled in 220 CE*)

mish**pat** (*justice*)

MISHPA**TIM** (*judgments, ordinances*)

mit**svot** (*commandments*)

Mit**zra**yim (*Egypt*)

miz**ra**chah (*on the east or sunward*)

m'la**chah** (*assigned tasks*)

m'le**chet** avo**dah** (*laborious work*)

M'na**sheh** (*Manasseh*)

m'no**rah** (*menorah, candelabra*)

Mo'**av** (*Moab*)

Mo**she** (*Moses*)

M'**rari** (*Merari*)

M'ri**vah** (*Meribah*)

m'shu**chim** (*anointed ones*)

M'**TSORA** (*infected one*)

Na**dav** (*Nadab*)

Naf**ta**li (*Naphtali*)

Nak**di**mon (*Nicodemus*)

na**sa** (*to lift up*)

na**si** (*lifted up one, exalted leader; i.e. chieftain/clan leader*)

NA**SO** (*elevate!*)

na**zir** (*consecrated, Nazirite*)

n'**chash** n'**cho**shet (*bronze serpent*)

N'**chush**tan (name for n'chash n'choshet/bronze serpent)

necha**lets** (*advance guard*)

ne**fesh** (*soul*)

Negev (southern region of Israel, from below the Dead Sea to Eilat)

ne**sech** (*drink*)

N'**filim** (*Nephilim*)

n'ki'**im** (*clear*, pl.)

niku**dot** (*dotted, pointed, punctuated*)

nil'**vu** go**yim** ra**bim** el A**DONAI** . . . v'**ha**yu li l'**am** (*many nations shall "be Levi" to the LORD . . . and become My people*)

Nisan (first month in the Hebrew calendar)

NO**ACH** (*Noah/rest*)

no**chri** (*temporary alien*)

no**fel** oo-g'**lui** ei**na**yim (*fallen prostrate and with uncovered eyes*)

No**vach** (*Nobah*)

n'si'**ei** ma**tot** avo**tam** (*exalted ones of their fathers' tribes*)

n'si'**im** (*tribal chieftains, clan leaders, exalted leaders; pl. of nasi*)

n'**tu**nim n'**tu**nim (*formally given over*)

nun (Hebrew letter for *n*)

Ohel Mo'ed (*Tent of Meeting*)
olah (*ascent offering; burnt or whole offering*)
olat tamid (*daily/regular ascent offering*)
olot (*ascent offerings*)
oo-l'fi he'alot he'anan (*whenever the cloud lifted up*)
ot (*sign*)
parah adumah (*reddish cow*)
parashah (Torah *portion*)
Parashat (*portion of _____*)
parashiot (Torah *portions*, pl.)
peh el-peh (*mouth to mouth*)
Pesach (*Passover*)
pidyon ha ben (*redemption of the firstborn*)
Pi haChirot (*the Mouth of Freedom*, Pi-hahiroth)
PINCHAS (*Phinehas/dark-skinned*)
p'kod . . . tif'k'dem ("*you shall most certainly count*")
P'KUDEI (*accountings of*)
P'lishtim (*Philistines*)
poiein ten aletheian (Grk. *to do the truth*; "keep the faith")
P'rushim (*Pharisees*)
P'tor (*Pethor*)
Ra'amses (*Rameses*)
Rachav (*Rahab*)
Radak (Rabbi David Kimchi)
Rambam (Rabbi Moshe ben Maimon, Maimonides)
Ramban (Rabbi Moshe ben Nachman, Nachmanides)
rashei alfei Yisra'el (*heads of the thousands of Israel*)
Rashi (Rabbi Shlomo ben Itzchak)
Rav (*Rabbi/Great One*)
rav-lachem (*too much to you!*)
Rav Sha'ul (*Paul*)
R'chov (*Rehob*)
reisheet (*first of*, referring to the foods "first processed")
reisheet arisoteichem challah (*first-processed of your dough, a round loaf*)
R'fidim (*Rephidim*)
rishon (*first*)
rishonim (*first generation*)
rosh (*head*)
rosh haP'or (*the summit/top of Peor*)
Rosh haShanah (*the Head of the Year*)
ruach (*wind, spirit*)
Ruach haKodesh (*Holy Spirit*)
R'uven (*Reuben*)
r'vi'i (*fourth*)
sachar (*wages*)
sarim rabim v'nichbadim me'eleh (*nobles, more of them and more honored than these*)
s'deh Tsofim al-rosh haPisgah (*field of Zophim on top of Pisgah*)
S'dom (*Sodom*)

Sefer B'MIDBAR (*Book of Numbers/in the wilderness*)

Sefer B'REISHEET (*Book of Genesis/in the beginning*)

Sefer D'VARIM (*Book of Deuteronomy/words*)

Sefer SH'MOT (*Book of Exodus/ names*)

Sefer VAYIKRA (*Book of Leviticus/then He called*)

Sephardic (pertaining to Sephardim, Jews of Spanish descent; abbrev. Seph.)

Shabbat (*Sabbath*)

shaked (*almond*)

Shappirah (*Sapphira/ Beautiful*)

Sha'ul (*Saul/Paul*)

Shavu'ot (lit. *weeks*, Feast of Weeks, Pentecost)

shemesh (*sun*)

sheni (*second*)

Sheol (see Sh'ol)

Shim'on (*Simeon*)

Shimshon (*Samson*)

shishi (*sixth*)

SH'LACH L'CHA (*send for yourself!*)

sh'lamim (*fellowhsip*)

shlishi (*third*)

Shlomo (*Solomon*)

SH'MINI (*eighth*)

Sh'mini Atseret (*eighth day of restraint,* last convocation day of the Torah, celebrated at the end of Sukkot; trans-

lated *concluding solemnity* in the Greek Septuagint (LXX))

SH'MOT (*names/Exodus*)

Sh'mu'el (*Samuel*)

shoked (*watches over*)

Sh'ol (*Sheol, abyss, grave, realm of the dead, underworld*)

shvi'i (*seventh*)

Sichon (*Sihon*)

sikim (*barbs*)

Simchat Torah (*joy of the Torah*)

Sivan (third month in the Hebrew calendar)

s'michah (*laying on of hands*)

spoudasomen (Greek for *let us make haste*, from the root form "spoudazo")

S'udat Adon (*the Lord's Supper*)

Sukkot (*Succoth, huts, booths*)

taf (*young, young male child*)

tafim (*young males,* pl. of taf)

talmidim (*students/disciples*)

Talmud (*commentary on the Mishnah*)

tamei (*ritually impure/contagious/defiled;* fem. tam'ah; pl. tam'u)

Tammuz (fourth month in the Hebrew calendar)

tam'u (*ritually impure ones*)

Tanakh (תנ״ך, *an acronym for the Hebrew canon; Torah, N'vi'im/Prophets, and K'tuvim/Writings*)

Tav'erah (*Taberah*/"burning")

TAZRIA (*she bears seed*)

t'chelet (*blue*)

Tetragrammaton, יהוה (*Yod-Hay-Vav-Hay; the four-letter name of* ADONAI)

tiftach ha'aretz et-piha vativla otam (*the earth opens her mouth and swallows them*)

timmei (*pollute, render impure*)

Tisha b'Av (*ninth of Av,* fast day commemorating the destruction of both Temples)

tis'u et-avon ha-mikdash (*they shall bear the sin of the sanctuary*)

t'nufah lifnei ADONAI (*elevated before the* LORD)

TOL'DOT (*generations, life story, offspring*)

Torah (*instruction*/Pentateuch, Gen.-Dt.)

T'RUMAH (*offering*)

t'rumat ADONAI (*contribution belonging to the* LORD*, lit. offering of* ADONAI)

t'rumot (*contributions*)

tsara'at (*skin affliction, infection,* scaly *skin disease,* sometimes translated *leprosy* from the Greek word *lepra*)

tsaru'a (*one suffering a skin affliction*)

TSAV (*command!*)

tsava (*work force*)

Tsin (*Zin*)

tsitsit (*tassel*; pl. tsitsiyot)

Ts'lof'chad (*Zelophehad*)

ts'ninim b'tsideichem (*spines in your sides*)

T'TSAVEH (*you shall command*)

Tziyon (*Zion*)

Tzor'ah (*Zorah*)

ulai yikareh ADONAI likrati (*perhaps the* LORD *will chance to call me*)

Uzi'el (*Uzziel*)

VAERA (*and I appeared*)

va-t'hi alav Ruach Elohim (*and the Spirit of God was upon him*)

vaya'alu (*and they went up*)

VAYAKHEL (*and he assembled*)

VAY'CHI (*and he lived*)

VAYERA (*and He appeared*)

vaYera k'vod-ADONAI el kol ha-edah! (*and appeared the Glory of God to all the congregation!*)

VAYESHEV (*and he settled*)

VAYETSE (*and he went out*)

vay'hi binso'a ha-aron (*when the ark would journey*)

vayichar-af Elohim . . . l'satan lo (*and the nostrils of God flared . . . to "Satan" him*)

VAYIGASH (*and he drew near*)

va-yikadesh bam (*and He was sanctified through them*)

vaYikar (*and happened upon*)
vaYikar Bil'am (*and Balaam happened upon*)
VAYIKRA (*and He called/ Numbers*)
vaYikra (*and he called*)
VAYIKRA ADONAI (*and the LORD called*)
VAYIKRA ADONAI el Moshe (*and the LORD called to Moses*)
VAYIKRA el-Moshe (*and He called to Moshe*)
VAYISHLACH (*and he sent*)
vaYishlach…mal'achim (*and he sent ahead . . . messengers/ angels*)
v'nasa (*and journey*)
v'nas'u et-z'nuteichem (*thus shall they bear your whoring*)
v'tsararu et-chem (*and they will assault you*)
ya'an lo he'e'mantem bi l'hakdisheni (*because you did not trust in Me to sanctify Me holy*)
Ya'azer (*Jazer*)
Yahtsah (*Jahaz*)
Ya'ir (*Jair*)
Yam Suf (*the Sea of Reeds*)
Yarden (*Jordan*)
Y'chezkel (*Ezekiel*)
Yesha'yahu (*Isaiah*)
Yeshua (*Jesus/salvation*)
Yeshua haMashiach (*Jesus the Messiah*)

Y'hoshua (*Joshua*)
Y'hudah (*Judah*)
Y'hudah haNasi (*Judah, the Leader*, compiler of Mishnah)
Yiftach (*Jephthah*)
yikar ADONAI el Bil'am (*the LORD happens upon Balaam*)
Yirm'yahu (*Jeremiah*)
yishma [Moshe] et-haKol (*Moses listened to the Voice*)
Yisra'el (*Israel*)
Yissakhar (*Issachar*)
YITRO (*Jethro/abundance*)
Yitzhar (*Izhar*)
Yizra'el (*God will sow*)
y'lidei ha-Anak . . . min ha-N'filim (*descendants of the giant from the original Titans*)
Y'recho (*Jericho*)
Y'rushalayim (*Jerusalem*)
zar (*stranger*)
zav (*one suffering from a bodily discharge*)
Z'charyah (*Zechariah*)
ziknei Mo'av v'Midyan (*elders of Moab and Midian*)
zot chukat hatorah (*this is the statute of the Torah/instruction*)
Z'vulun (*Zebulun*)
יהוה (See *Tetragrammaton*.)
תנ״ך (If verse numbers vary, Hebrew references show this symbol. See *Tanakh*.)

Bibliography

Abarbanel, Isaac ben Judah, also Abravanel. See Stone Edition, Scherman, Rabbi Nosson (Gen. Ed.).

Alcalay, Reuben. *The Complete English-Hebrew, Hebrew-English Dictionary*. Ramat Gan: Massadah Publishing Co., 1981.

Alter, Robert. *The Art of Biblical Narrative*. Berkeley, CA: Basic Books, 1981.

Ashley, Timothy R. *The Book of Numbers*. In R. K. Harrison and Robert L. Hubbard, Jr. (Gen. Eds.), *The New International Commentary on the Old Testament*. Grand Rapids, MI: Wm B. Eerdmans Publ. Co., 1993.

Attridge, Harold W. *The Epistle to the Hebrews*. In Helmut Koester (Gen. Ed.), *Hermeneia*. Philadelphia: Fortress Press, 1989.

Avot, Pirkei Avot, see *The Metsudah Pirkei Avos: The Wisdom of the Fathers*.

Baraita, D'melechet haMishkan, 13, cited in Ramban

Barrett, C. K. *The Gospel According to St. John: An Introduction with Commentary and Notes on the Greek Text*. Second Edition. Philadelphia: The Westminster Press, 1978.

Bava Kamma, see Schorr, *Talmud Bavli*.

Bav. Metzia, see Schorr, *Talmud Bavli*.

B. B., Bava Basra, see Schorr, *Talmud Bavli*.

Beasley-Murray, George R. In David R. Hubbard and Glen W. Barker (Gen. Eds.), *Word Biblical Commentary*. Volume 36. *John*. Waco, TX: Word Books, 1987.

Ben-Abba, Dov. *Signet Hebrew-English English-Hebrew Dictionary*. Massada-Press/Modan Publishing House Ltd., Israel, 1977.

Ben Avraham, Rabbi Alexander, and Sharfman, Rabbi Benjamin (Eds.). *The Pentateuch and Rashi's Commentary*. Brooklyn, NY: S. S. & R. Publishing Company, Inc. (also Philadelphia: Press of the Jewish Publication Society), 1976.

Ber., Berachot, see Schorr, *Talmud Bavli*.

Beshallach, Beshallah, see Mekhilta.

Birnbaum, Philip. *Encyclopedia of Jewish Concepts.* NY: Hebrew Publishing Company, 1993.

Birnbaum, Philip (Ed.). *Maimonides' Mishneh Torah.* New York: Hebrew Publishing Co., 1985.

Blackman, Philip (Ed.). *Mishnayoth.* Gateshead: Judaica Press, Ltd., 1983.

Brown, Raymond E. *The Gospel According to John. The Anchor Bible.* Volumes 29, 29A. Garden City, NY: Doubleday and Company, Inc., 1984.

Bruce, F. F. *The Epistle to the Hebrews.* In F. F. Bruce (Gen. Ed.), *The New International Commentary on the New Testament.* Grand Rapids, MI: Wm. B. Eerdmans Publishing Company, 1979.

Budd, Philip J. In David R. Hubbard and Glen W. Barker (Gen. Eds.), *Word Biblical Commentary.* Volume 5. *Numbers.* Waco, TX: Word Books, 1984.

Bullinger, E. W. *Figures of Speech Used in the Bible.* Grand Rapids, MI: Baker Book House, 1987. (Original work published in 1898).

Carson, D. A. *Exegetical Fallacies.* Grand Rapids, MI, Baker Book House, 1984.

Childs, Brevard S. *Biblical Theology of the Old and New Testaments: Theological Reflection on the Christian Bible.* Minneapolis: Fortress Press, 1993.

Cohen, A. (Gen. Ed.). *Soncino Books of the Bible.* Volumes 1-14. London: The Soncino Press Limited, 1978.

Concordance to the Novum Testamentum Graece. Third edition. Berlin: Walter De Gruyter, 1987.

Douglas, Mary. *In the Wilderness: The Doctrine of Defilement in the Book of Numbers.* David J. A. Clines and Philip R. Davies (Eds.). Journal for the Study of the Old Testament. Supplement Series 158. Sheffield: JSOT Press, 1993.

Douglas, Mary. *Numbers as Literature.* Oxford: Oxford University Press, 1999.

Drazin, Israel. *Targum Onkelos to Numbers: an English Translation of the Text with Analysis and Commentary* (Based on the A. Sperber and A. Berliner Editions). University of Denver: Center for Judaic Studies, 1994.

Driver, S. R., Plummer, A., and Briggs, C. A. (Gen. Eds.). *The International Critical Commentary on the Holy Scriptures of the Old and New Testaments.* Edinburgh: T. & T. Clark, 1979. (Original work published 1896-1924).

Ellingworth, Paul. *The Epistle to the Hebrews.* In I. Howard Marshall and W. Ward Gasque (Gen. Eds.), *The New International Greek New Testament Commentary.* Grand Rapids, MI: William B. Eerdmans Publishing Company, 1993.

Elwell, W. A. (Ed.). *Evangelical Dictionary of Theology.* Grand Rapids, MI: Baker Book House, 1984.

Evans, Louis H., Jr. *Hebrews.* In Lloyd J. Ogilvie (Gen. Ed.), *The Communicator's Commentary.* Dallas: Word Publishing, 1985.

Even-Shoshan, Avraham (Ed.). *New Concordance for the Torah, Prophets, and Writings.* Jerusalem: Sivan Press, 1977.

Feinberg, Jeffrey Enoch. *Walk Exodus!* Baltimore: Messianic Jewish Publishers, 1999.

Feinberg, Jeffrey Enoch. *Walk Genesis!* Baltimore: Messianic Jewish Publishers, 1998.

Feinberg, Jeffrey Enoch. *Walk Leviticus!* Baltimore: Messianic Jewish Publishers, 2001.

Feinberg, Pat. *Jot & Tittle.* Littleton, CO: First Fruits of Zion, Inc., 1998.

Feinberg, Pat. *Search the Sidra.* Littleton, CO: First Fruits of Zion, Inc., 2001.

Fisch, S. *Ezekiel.* In A. Cohen (Gen. Ed.), *The Soncino Books of the Bible.* Volume 7. London: The Soncino Press, Ltd., 1978.

Fox, Everett. *The Schocken Bible: The Five Books of Moses.* Volume 1. New York: Schocken Books, 1995.

Frankel, Ellen and Teutsch, Betsy P. (1992). *The Encyclopedia of Jewish Symbols.* Northvale, NJ: Jason Aronson, 1992.

Friedman, Rabbi Alexander Zusia. *Wellsprings of Torah.* Transl.

by Gertrude Hirschler. New York: Judaica Press, Inc., 1990.

Gellis, Maurice and Gribetz, Dennis. *The Glory of Torah Reading.* Revised edition. Monsey, NY: M.P. Press, Inc., 1996.

Ginzberg, Louis. *The Legends of the Jews.* Volume 2. Transl. by Henrietta Szold. Baltimore: The Johns Hopkins University Press, 1998.

Gray, George Buchanan. *The International Critical Commentary: Numbers.* New York: Charles Scribner's Sons, 1903.

Gundry, Robert H. *Matthew: A Commentary on his Literary and Theological Art.* Grand Rapids, MI: Wm. B. Eerdmans Publishing Company, 1982.

Herczeg, Rabbi Yisra'el Isser Zvi (Ed.). *The Torah: With Rashi's Commentary Translated, Annotated, and Elucidated.* Artscroll Series/The Sapirstein Edition. Brooklyn: Mesorah Publications, Ltd., 1995.

Hertz, Dr. J. H. (Ed.). *The Pentateuch and Haftorahs.* Second edition. London: Soncino Press, 1975.

Heschel, Abraham J. *The Prophets.* Volume 1. NY: Harper and Row, Publishers, 1969.

Hilton, Rabbi Michael and Marshall, Fr. Gordion. *The Gospels & Rabbinic Judaism: A Study Guide.* Hoboken, NJ: KTAV, 1988.

Hirsch, Samson Raphael, Trans. *The Pentateuch, Haftarah, and the Five Megillot.* Ed. by Ephraim Oratz. New York: The Judaica Press, Inc., 1990. (English translation by Gertrude Hirschler; German work published in 1867-1878).

Ibn Ezra, see Schorr, *Talmud Bavli.*

ibn Paquda, R. Bachya. *Duties of the Heart.* Transl. by Moses Hyamson. Jerusalem: Feldheim Publishers, 1986. (Translated from Arabic into Hebrew by R. Yehuda Ibn Tibbon).

JPS, Jewish Publication Society, see *Tanakh: The Holy Scriptures.*

Kahan, Rabbi Aharon. *The Taryag Mitzvos.* Brooklyn: Keser Torah Pub., 1988. (Based on the classical *Sefer haChinuch*).

Kantor, Mattis. *The Jewish Time Line Encyclopedia: A Year-by-Year History from Creation to the Present.* Northvale, NJ: Jason Aronson, Inc., 1989.

Keil, C. F. and Delitzsch, F. *Commentary on the Old Testament.* Transl. by James Martin. Volumes 1-10. Grand Rapids, MI: William B. Eerdmans Publishing Company, 1976.

Kent, Homer A. *The Epistle to the Hebrews.* Grand Rapids, MI: Baker Book House, 1985.

Kohlenberger, John R. III (Ed.). *The NIV Interlinear Hebrew-English Old Testament.* Grand Rapids, MI: Zondervan Publishing House, 1979.

Kolatch, Alfred J. *The Complete Dictionary of English and Hebrew First Names.* Middle Village, NY: Jonathan David Publishers, Inc., 1984.

Lachs, Samuel Tobias. *A Rabbinic Commentary on the New Testament.* Hoboken, NJ: KTAV Publishing House, Inc., 1987.

Lane, William L. *Hebrews: A Call to Commitment.* Peabody, MA: Hendrickson Publishers, 1988.

Lane, William L. *Word Biblical Commentary: Hebrews 1-13.* Volumes 47a, 47b. Waco, TX: Word Books, Publisher, 1991.

Leibowitz, Nehama. *Studies in Bamidbar (Numbers).* Transl. by Aryeh Newman. Revised edition. Jerusalem: Hemed Press, 1982.

Levine, Baruch A. *Numbers 1-20. The Anchor Bible.* NY: Doubleday, a division of Bantam Doubleday Dell Publishing Group, Inc., 1993.

Levine, Baruch A. *Numbers 21-36. The Anchor Bible.* NY: Doubleday, a division of Random House, Inc., 2000.

Longenecker, Richard N. *Acts.* In Frank E. Gaebelein (Gen. Ed.). *The Expositor's Bible Commentary.* Vol. 9. Grand Rapids: Zondervan, 1981.

Martin, Ralph P. *James.* In David A. Hubbard and Glenn W. Barker (Gen. Eds.), *Word Biblical Commentary.* Volume 48. Waco, TX: Word Books, Publisher, 1988.

Mekhilta According to Rabbi Ishmael: An Analytical Translation. Transl. by Jacob Neusner. Volume 1. Atlanta: Scholars Press, Brown Judaic Studies, 1988.

Mekhilta, Beshallah, see *Mekhilta,* Vol. 1.

The Metsudah Pirkei Avos: The Wisdom of the Fathers. Selected and translated by Rabbi Avrohom Davis. New York: Metsudah Publications, 1986.

Midrash Tanchuma. See Townsend, John T.

Milgrom, Jacob. *The JPS Torah Commentary: Numbers.* Philadelphia: The Jewish Publication Society, 1990.

MK, Moed Kattan, see Schorr, *Talmud Bavli.*

Morris, Leon. *The Gospel According to John.* In F. F. Bruce (Gen. Ed.), *The New International Commentary on the New Testament.* Grand Rapids, MI: Wm B. Eerdmans Publ. Co., 1979.

Munk, Rabbi Elie. *The Call of the Torah: An Anthology of Interpretation and Commentary on the Five Books of Moses: BAMIDBAR.* Translated from the French by E. S. Mazer. Edited by Yitzchok Kirzner. In R. Nosson Scherman and R. Meir Zlotowitz (Eds.), *ArtScroll Mesorah Series.* Brooklyn, NY: Mesorah Publications, Ltd., 1993.

M. Yoma, Mishnah Yoma, see Blackman, *Mishnayoth.*

Nachshoni, Yehuda. *Studies in the Weekly Parashah.* Transl. by Raphael Blumberg and Yaakov Petroff. Volume 4: Bamidbar. Brooklyn: Mesorah Publications, Ltd., 1989.

Ned., Nedarim, see Schorr, *Talmud Bavli.*

Neusner, Jacob. *Sifre to Numbers: an American Translation and Explanation.* Volume 1, Sifre to Numbers 1-58. Brown Judaic Studies 118. Atlanta: Scholars Press, 1986.

Neusner, Jacob. *Sifre to Numbers: an American Translation and Explanation.* Volume 2, Sifre to Numbers 59-115. Brown Judaic Studies 119. Atlanta: Scholars Press, 1986.

The New English Bible. Standard edition. New York: Oxford University Press, 1971.

Novum Testamentum Graece. Nestle-Aland Edition. Stuttgart: Deutsche Bibelstiftung, 1981.

Num. R., Numbers Rabbah, see *Soncino Midrash Rabbah.*

Oppen, Menachem Moshe. *The Yom Kippur Avodah.* The Pictorial Avodah Series. C.I. S. Distributors. Baltimore: M'chon Harbotzas Torah, Inc., Chicago: Chicago Community Kollel, 1988.

ORT, *Navigating the Bible: Interactive Bar/Bat Mitzvah CD-Rom.* Sung by Cantor Moshe Haschel. London: World ORT Union, 1998.

Ouaknin, Marc-Alain. *The Burnt Book: Reading the Talmud.* Transl. by Llewellyn Brown. Princeton: Princeton University Press, 1995.

Plaut, W. Gunther. *The Haftarah Commentary.* Transl. by Chaim Stern. New York: UAHC Press, 1996.

Raban, Abraham ben Nathan of Lunel, 12th century. *Sefer Hamanhig,* Hilchot Ta'anit, #16, see Plaut.

Radak, Rabbi David Kimchi. See Schorr, *Talmud Bavli.*

Rambam, see Birnbaum, *Maimonides' Mishneh Torah.*

Ramban (Nachmanides), Commentary on the Torah: Numbers. Transl. by Rabbi Dr. Charles B. Chavel. NY: Shilo Publishing House, 1975.

Rashi. See Ben Avraham, Rabbi Abraham et al. or Herczek, Rabbi Yisra'el Isser Zvi.

R.H., Rosh HaShannah, see Schorr, *Talmud Bavli.*

Robertson, A. T. *Word Pictures in the New Testament.* Grand Rapids, MI: Baker Book House, 1932.

Sanh., Sanhedrin, see Schorr, *Talmud Bavli.*

Sailhamer, John H. *The Pentateuch as Narrative.* Grand Rapids, MI: Zondervan Publishing House, 1992.

Scherman, Rabbi Nosson (Gen. Ed.). *The Chumash: The Torah, Haftaros, and Five Megillos with a Commentary Anthologized from the Rabbinic Writings.* Ed. by Rabbi Hersh Goldwurn, Rabbi Avie Gold, and Rabbi Meir Zlotowitz. Artscroll Series, The Stone Edition. Brooklyn: Mesorah Publications, Ltd., 1995.

Schorr, Rabbi Yisroel Simcha (Gen. Ed.). *Talmud Bavli.* The Artscroll Series, Schottenstein Edition. Brooklyn: Mesorah Publications, Ltd., 1993.

Sed. Olam, *Seder Olam: The Rabbinic View of Biblical Chronology.* Transl. by Heinrich W. Guggenheimer. Northvale, NJ: Jason Aronson Inc., 1998.

Sforno, Ovadiah. *Commentary on the Torah.* Transl. by Rabbi

Raphael Pelcovitz. The Artscroll Mesorah Series. Brooklyn: Mesorah Publications, Ltd., 1997.

Shabb., Shabbos, see Schorr, *Talmud Bavli*.

Shev., Shevuos, see Schorr, *Talmud Bavli*.

Shulman, Eliezer. *The Sequence of Events in the Old Testament*. Transl. by Sarah Lederhendler. Fifth edition. Jerusalem: Investment Co. of Bank Hapoalim and Ministry of Defense— Publishing House, 1987.

Sifre, Sifrei, see Neusner, Jacob.

Soncino, see A. Cohen (Ed.), *The Soncino Books of the Bible*.

Sot., Sotah, see Schorr, *Talmud Bavli*.

The Soncino Midrash Rabbah. The CD Rom Judaic Classics Library. Distributed by Davka Corporation. Brooklyn, NY: Soncino Press, 1983.

Stern, David H., Trans. *Complete Jewish Bible*. Clarksville, MD: Jewish New Testament Publications, 1998.

Stern, David H. *Jewish New Testament Commentary*. Clarksville, MD: Jewish New Testament Publications, 1992.

Stone Edition, see Scherman, Rabbi Nosson (Gen. Ed.).

Sukk., Sukkot, see Schorr, *Talmud Bavli*.

Taan., Taanis, see Schorr, *Talmud Bavli*.

Talmud, see Schorr, *Talmud Bavli*.

Tanakh: The Holy Scriptures. Philadelphia: Jewish Publication Society, 1988.

Tanch., Tanchuma or Tanhuma, see Townsend, *Midrash Tanhuma*.

Targum Onkelos. See Drazin, Israel.

Tenney, Merrill C. *John*. Volume 9. Grand Rapids, MI: Zondervan Publishing House, 1981.

Ter., Terumoth, see Blackman, *Mishnayoth*.

Tikkun Kor'im haM'fuar. Brooklyn, NY: Im haSefer, 1994.

Tos. haRosh.,

Townsend, John T. *Midrash Tanhuma*. Translated into English with Indices and Brief Notes (S. Buber Recension). Hoboken, NY: KTAV Publishing House, 1997.

Unger, Merrill F. (Ed.). *Unger's Bible Dictionary*. Chicago: Moody Press, 1979.

Walk Exodus!, see Feinberg.

Walk Genesis!, see Feinberg.

Walk Leviticus!, see Feinberg.

Werblowsky, Dr. R. J. Zwi and Wigoder, Dr. Geoffrey (Eds.). *The Encyclopedia of the Jewish Religion*. Jerusalem: Masada, 1967.

Wigram, George V. *The Englishman's Hebrew and Chaldee Concordance of the Old Testament*. Grand Rapids, MI: Baker Book House, 1980. (Original work published in 1843).

The Works of Josephus. Transl. by William Whiston. Lynn, MA: Hendrickson Publishers, 1980.

Yad, Ned., see Birnbaum, *Maimonides' Mishneh Torah*.

Yad, Par. Adum., see Birnbaum, *Maimonides' Mishneh Torah*.

Yoma, see Schorr, *Talmud Bavli*.

Zav., Zavim, see Blackman, *Mishnayoth*.